An Analysis of

Michel Foucault's

What is an Author?

Tim Smith-Laing

Published by Macat International Ltd
24:13 Coda Centre, 189 Munster Road, London SW6 6AW.

Distributed exclusively by Routledge
2 Park Square, Milton Park, Abingdon, Oxon OX14 4RN
711 Third Avenue, New York, NY 10017, USA

Routledge is an imprint of the Taylor & Francis Group, an informa business

www.macat.com
info@macat.com

Cataloguing in Publication Data
A catalogue record for this book is available from the British Library.
Library of Congress Cataloguing-in-Publication Data is available upon request.
Cover illustration: Angus Greig

ISBN 978-1-912453-53-5 (hardback)
ISBN 978-1-912453-08-5 (paperback)
ISBN 978-1-912453-23-8 (e-book)

Notice
The information in this book is designed to orientate readers of the work under analysis,
to elucidate and contextualise its key ideas and themes, and to aid in the development
of critical thinking skills. It is not meant to be used, nor should it be used, as a
substitute for original thinking or in place of original writing or research. References and
notes are provided for informational purposes and their presence does not constitute
endorsement of the information or opinions therein. This book is presented solely for
educational purposes. It is sold on the understanding that the publisher is not engaged
to provide any scholarly advice. The publisher has made every effort to ensure that
this book is accurate and up-to-date, but makes no warranties or representations with
regard to the completeness or reliability of the information it contains. The information
and the opinions provided herein are not guaranteed or warranted to produce particular
results and may not be suitable for students of every ability. The publisher shall not be
liable for any loss, damage or disruption arising from any errors or omissions, or from
the use of this book, including, but not limited to, special, incidental, consequential or
other damages caused, or alleged to have been caused, directly or indirectly, by the
information contained within.

CONTENTS

THE MACAT LIBRARY

The Macat Library is a series of unique academic explorations of seminal works in the humanities and social sciences – books and papers that have had a significant and widely recognised impact on their disciplines. It has been created to serve as much more than just a summary of what lies between the covers of a great book. It illuminates and explores the influences on, ideas of, and impact of that book. Our goal is to offer a learning resource that encourages critical thinking and fosters a better, deeper understanding of important ideas.

Each publication is divided into three Sections: Influences, Ideas, and Impact. Each Section has four Modules. These explore every important facet of the work, and the responses to it.

This Section-Module structure makes a Macat Library book easy to use, but it has another important feature. Because each Macat book is written to the same format, it is possible (and encouraged!) to cross-reference multiple Macat books along the same lines of inquiry or research. This allows the reader to open up interesting interdisciplinary pathways.

To further aid your reading, lists of glossary terms and people mentioned are included at the end of this book (these are indicated by an asterisk [*] throughout) – as well as a list of works cited.

Macat has worked with the University of Cambridge to identify the elements of critical thinking and understand the ways in which six different skills combine to enable effective thinking.
Three allow us to fully understand a problem; three more give us the tools to solve it. Together, these six skills make up the **PACIER** model of critical thinking. They are:

ANALYSIS – understanding how an argument is built
EVALUATION – exploring the strengths and weaknesses of an argument
INTERPRETATION – understanding issues of meaning

CREATIVE THINKING – coming up with new ideas and fresh connections
PROBLEM-SOLVING – producing strong solutions
REASONING – creating strong arguments

To find out more, visit **WWW.MACAT.COM.**

CRITICAL THINKING AND "WHAT IS AN AUTHOR?"

Primary critical thinking skill: CREATIVE THINKING
Secondary critical thinking skill: INTERPRETATION

A central theme in Michel Foucault's work is the quest to see through the surface of society and understand the processes going on beneath it. Across a long career which saw him become perhaps the most influential philosopher of the mid-late twentieth century, he applied his efforts to analyzing a range of phenomena and their relationship to power and the individual in society. These analyses ranged from the history of mental illness and its classification, to the history of crime and punishment, through to the history of human sexuality.

His 1969 essay "What is an Author?" applies the same approach to the central figure of literary criticism: the author. It asks, contrary to traditional thought, whether an author is truly the real individual who writes a text. The essay exemplifies the application of creative thinking to a difficult problem in that it turns traditional notions of authorship inside out. Like all good creative thinkers, Foucault makes new connections, sees things from new angles, redefines the issues at stake, and generates new hypotheses. Underlying this process is Foucault's skill as an interpreter. "What is an Author?" pursues creative thinking through a careful process of looking at historical evidence to clarify the true meaning of the term "author."

ABOUT THE AUTHOR OF THE ORIGINAL WORK

The French philosopher and historian **Michel Foucault** was one of the most influential figures in twentieth century thought. Born in 1926 in Poitiers, France, he was a central player in the development of "French theory"—a loosely affiliated intellectual movement of iconoclastic thinkers working in 1960s Paris, whose work reverberated through university departments across the world from the 1970s onwards. Foucault was a pioneering analyst of hidden and repressed histories whose work, in his own words, sought to "show up, transform, and reverse the systems which quietly order us about"—the invisible structures that confine and define us as humans.

Along with the short, influential "What is an Author?" (1969), Foucault was the author of a number of seminal texts including *The History of Madness* (1961), *The Order of Things* (1966), *Archaeology of Knowledge* (1969), *Discipline and Punish* (1975), and *The History of Sexuality* (1976-1984). Through these he came to be known as the greatest analyst of the interactions between power and social life, consistently unsettling our deepest assumptions about what is true, real, or natural. By the time of his death from complications of AIDS in 1984 he was widely recognized as the most influential thinker in the world.

ABOUT THE AUTHOR OF THE ANALYSIS

Dr Tim Smith-Laing took his DPhil in English literature at Merton College, Oxford, and has held positions at Jesus College, Oxford, and Sciences Po in Paris.

ABOUT MACAT

GREAT WORKS FOR CRITICAL THINKING

Macat is focused on making the ideas of the world's great thinkers accessible and comprehensible to everybody, everywhere, in ways that promote the development of enhanced critical thinking skills.

It works with leading academics from the world's top universities to produce new analyses that focus on the ideas and the impact of the most influential works ever written across a wide variety of academic disciplines. Each of the works that sit at the heart of its growing library is an enduring example of great thinking. But by setting them in context – and looking at the influences that shaped their authors, as well as the responses they provoked – Macat encourages readers to look at these classics and game-changers with fresh eyes. Readers learn to think, engage and challenge their ideas, rather than simply accepting them.

'Macat offers an amazing first-of-its-kind tool for interdisciplinary learning and research. Its focus on works that transformed their disciplines and its rigorous approach, drawing on the world's leading experts and educational institutions, opens up a world-class education to anyone.'

Andreas Schleicher
Director for Education and Skills, Organisation for Economic Co-operation and Development

'Macat is taking on some of the major challenges in university education ... They have drawn together a strong team of active academics who are producing teaching materials that are novel in the breadth of their approach.'

Prof Lord Broers,
former Vice-Chancellor of the University of Cambridge

'The Macat vision is exceptionally exciting. It focuses upon new modes of learning which analyse and explain seminal texts which have profoundly influenced world thinking and so social and economic development. It promotes the kind of critical thinking which is essential for any society and economy. This is the learning of the future.'

Rt Hon Charles Clarke, former UK Secretary of State for Education

'The Macat analyses provide immediate access to the critical conversation surrounding the books that have shaped their respective discipline, which will make them an invaluable resource to all of those, students and teachers, working in the field.'

Professor William Tronzo, University of California at San Diego

WAYS IN TO THE TEXT

KEY POINTS

- Michel Foucault (1926-1984) was a French philosopher and historian.
- "What is an Author?" is an essay that suggests a new way of looking at the place of the author in relation to the meaning of texts.
- "What is an Author?" plots a way between author-centered and reader-centered theories of meaning.

Who Is Michel Foucault?

Michel Foucault was born in Poitiers, France in 1926. After graduating from his *lycée** (high-school), he entered the competitive classes for admission to one of France's most prestigious higher education institutions, the École Normale Supérieure (ENS).* There he studied under and alongside some of the most important thinkers of his time. He initially gained a degree in psychology, while also receiving training in history and philosophy. He later went on to teach psychology at the ENS, before going on to other institutions including the University of California, Berkeley.

In the early part of his career, much of Foucault's work examined the history of medicine. From the mid-1950s he was known for his critical work on the history of madness, its diagnosis, and its treatment. His central interest throughout his career was the relationship between power and knowledge in society, and how it affects the lives of individuals. "What is an Author?" was written and presented as a lecture in France in 1969. By this point in his career, Foucault had turned to more general analyses of knowledge and power in society through the idea of discourse,* which he examined in his work from the mid-1960s onwards. Later, his work extended to examine the history of prisons and punishment, and the history of sexuality.

From the late 1970s onwards, Foucault was perhaps the most famous philosopher and public intellectual in the world. Through translations and his lectures at Berkeley, his work became well known in the United States where it helped revolutionize the fields of humanities and social sciences. Credited as a formative influence on the schools of New Historicism* and Queer Theory,* Foucault is recognized as one of "the most influential thinkers of the latter [sic] twentieth century."[1]

What Does "What is an Author?" Say?

"What is an Author?" is one of Foucault's few works directly applicable to literary theory. Its central argument is that critics and historians should not focus their attention on finding out what an author wanted to communicate in a text. Instead, they should focus on how the social and legal conditions of specific societies influence and control the relationship between texts and their writers. For Foucault, texts, authors, and the idea of the author are closely related to the way power circulates in societies—or more simply, how societies exert control on human beings.

This emphasis stems from the initial argument that we cannot know exactly what an author intended—even if the author themselves knew what they intended—and that this cannot, therefore, be the "true meaning" of a text. Other critics had taken this stance before Foucault. Notably his friend Roland Barthes* had argued that meaning was created by readers, *not* authors, and thus famously pronounced "the death of the author."* This was a controversial stance that stirred up considerable debate at the time.

Foucault's essay works from a similar starting point as Barthes's idea, but reaches a different conclusion. For Foucault, what is interesting is that, despite the reader's role in creating meaning, we give texts "authors" anyway. Indeed, as he puts it, some kinds of texts demand authors, or come equipped with what he terms an "author function."* That is, they come with assigned authors whom we regard as "responsible" for the work, and whom we tend to construct as living, breathing human beings. Crucially, however, they are precisely not real human beings, but, rather, a function of certain social processes.

"What is an Author?" focuses on these social processes and on the "author function." The essay asks, in an open-ended way, when society first felt the need to assign texts to authors, and why. It then goes on to ask what kinds of texts are equipped with an "author function," and what that function does for them. Finally, Foucault asks whether there are other kinds of discourse that can be said to have authors or author functions.

Foucault's central suggestion regarding these questions is that texts and their meanings become tied to authors in order for states to be able to exert power over them. That is, texts are legally attributed to authors in order for states to be able to hold authors responsible for their words. By this mechanism, states can make sure that writers do not contradict or unsettle social structures. The author is, therefore, a function used to control texts as they circulate, and is, as a result, linked to how power permeates society.

This is a crucial theme throughout Foucault's work: the way in which seemingly natural social processes and apparently "natural" or "instinctive" assumptions are in fact "socially constructed,"— generated and, as it were, bred into us by society.

Why Does "What is an Author?" Matter?

"What is an Author?" matters for two overriding reasons: as an introduction to a key issue in literary theory, and as an introduction to Michel Foucault's work and thought in general. Foucault is without a doubt one of the most significant and influential thinkers of the twentieth century. His critiques of how power functions in society have informed political movements across the world, particularly among feminist* and LBGTQ* movements. His work has also had a transformative impact across the fields of humanities and social sciences.[2] On that count alone, "What is an Author?" is a key text for students of literature.

Authorial intention* remains a central topic in literature courses. It comes down to a truly fundamental question in the field: What do we mean by "the meaning of a text"? Many newcomers to literary analysis are perhaps likely to answer: "What an author intended it to mean." But this opens up a whole set of questions:

- Do authors know what they intend?
- What about unintended meanings?
- What about meanings that change across history?
- How can we know what an author intended?

After all, intention is not a simple concept. We ourselves do not always know what we mean, in the fullest sense of the term. Additionally, we very often cannot tell what others mean, even in apparently simple communications.

These questions cut to the heart of what literary analysis tries to do. Often, it is about trying to reconstruct authorial intention, and therefore it needs to have an awareness of the difficulties of that process. Foucault's essay alerts us to those difficulties in a way that all students can benefit from.

More than that, it also offers other possibilities for what we can do when analyzing texts. Texts and discourses, Foucault argues, tell us important things about the societies they come from. In particular, they tell us about how knowledge and power interact with each other and with human individuals in those societies. His argument is that this is the most important thing to analyze. Evenmore, that it is precisely in the ideas that seem most natural (e.g. texts have authors) that we can trace the workings of social and power structures. By questioning the idea of the author, Foucault is asking his readers to look closely at the assumptions of their society.

NOTES

1   C. G. Prado, "Editor's introduction" in C. G. Prado ed. *Foucault's Legacy,* (London: Continuum, 2009), 1.

2   For a summary of Foucault's wide-ranging impact, see Prado, "Editor's Introduction", passim.

SECTION 1
INFLUENCES

THE AUTHOR AND THE HISTORICAL CONTEXT

KEY POINTS

- "What is an Author?" is one of the most important short texts dealing with the status of the author in literary criticism.
- The argument of "What is an Author?" is shaped by Michel Foucault's interest in the relationship between history and human thought over time.
- "What is an Author?" springs directly from Foucault's relationships with other key thinkers in 1960s France, particularly Roland Barthes.

Why Read This Text?

Michel Foucault's "What is an Author?" is a classic text in literary theory and practice. Originally presented as a lecture to the Société française de philosophie* on February 22, 1969, it is still taught and read as a contribution to conceptual investigations of the author. Often read alongside William K. Wimsatt* and Monroe C. Beardsley's* "The Intentional Fallacy"* (1946) and Roland Barthes's "The Death of the Author" (1968), it is a standard text in introductory courses on literary theory.

Beyond the issues surrounding authors in literary criticism, "What is an Author?" is a superb gateway for readers who want to expand their horizons in literary theory more generally. It can be traced as in important text for later trends, particularly New Historicism. On account of its length and relatively self-contained arguments, it also serves as an approachable introduction to the rest of Foucault's work.

> **❝ In a sense […] all the rest of my life I've been trying to do intellectual things that would attract beautiful boys. ❞**
>
> Michel Foucault, quoted in James Miller, *The Passion of Michel Foucault*

As one of the most significant thinkers of the second half of the twentieth century, Foucault's influence extends across intellectual history, literary criticism, philosophy, and sociology. Sooner or later, most students in the humanities and social sciences find themselves needing to have some familiarity with his thought. "What is an Author?" is an excellent starting point.

Author's Life

Michel Foucault was born Paul-Michel Foucault on October 15, 1926, in Poitiers, France. His parents, Dr. Paul-André Foucault and Anne Malapert, were both from medical families. Foucault was expected to enter medicine, but by the age of 10 he had already decided to become a historian.[1]

Foucault continued his schooling during the German occupation of France in World War II. In 1943, he took the preparatory classes required for entrance to the highest level of France's university system, the *grandes écoles*. In 1946, he finally succeeded in the examinations for Paris's École Normale Supérieure (ENS), perhaps France's most prestigious educational institution.

Despite struggling with depression (associated partly with coming to terms with his homosexuality), Foucault was successful at the ENS, gaining qualifications in philosophy and psychology. In 1951, he began tutoring in psychology there himself, before researching and teaching elsewhere in France and in various posts abroad. In 1961, he published his first major book *Folie et Déraison*.[2] Both acclaimed and criticized, it helped Foucault rise to prominence in France.

Foucault further developed the themes of *Folie et Déraison* with *Naissance de la clinique* (1963),[3] before turning to broader intellectual history in *Les mots et les choses* (1966).[4] As his public and academic profile rose, he also became increasingly involved with left-wing politics and student movements in France and Tunisia, and advocated for French prison reform.

In 1969, Foucault presented "What is an Author?" and published *L'Archéologie du savoir*, before being appointed professor of philosophy at the new, experimental University of Vincennes.[5] In 1970, he was elected to the Collège de France*—one of the greatest accolades accorded by French academia. From the 1970s until his death, Foucault was one of the most prominent intellectuals in the world.

Foucault dedicated the last 15 years of his life to examining the history of prisons and punishment (*Surveiller et punir*, 1975),[6] and analyzing notions of sexuality across time (*Histoire de la sexualité*; three volumes, 1976, 1984, 1984).[7] He died from complications of AIDS in Paris on June 25, 1984.

Author's Background

The focus of "What is an Author?" on the overlap between literary theory and state power bears witness to French politics at the time. It is important to bear in mind Foucault's overall fascination with state power and legal authoritarianism. These were live issues, as France suffered multiple political crises throughout the 1950s and 60s. Despite the establishment of a new constitution in 1946, these decades saw French politics repeatedly torn between reactionary and radical movements tussling over the future of the country and its colonial possessions.

Perhaps the most psychologically significant events of the time were the Algerian War* (1958-1962) and the student protests of May 1968.* The former saw the struggle for Algerian independence erupt into civil war with brutal intervention from the French military.

Within France, the war created threats of a military coup and caused the government to collapse. This was followed by the establishment of a new constitution in 1958. The new government had a military figure at its head: General Charles de Gaulle,* the hero of the French Liberation* in 1945.

Though decolonization* accelerated from 1960, radical movements still clashed with the French state. In 1968, after the French Communist Party (PCF)* and French Socialists* united to oust de Gaulle, left-wing student demonstrations erupted in Paris. With violent clashes between police and protesters, the crisis spread and caused the government to shut down. Though de Gaulle and his allies won elections in June 1968, political instability continued. De Gaulle resigned in April 1969, just two months after Foucault presented "What is an Author?"

None of this escaped Foucault, who from the 1950s onwards was deeply involved with left-wing and student political movements. Like many intellectuals, Foucault joined the PCF. Though he resigned his membership after three years, he remained active on the Left, and was deeply opposed to state violence and authoritarianism.[8] His commitment is visible throughout his work, including in "What is an Author?"

NOTES

1   For a detailed chronological outline of Foucault's life, see Daniel Defert, "Chronology" in *A Companion to Foucault* eds. Christopher Falzon, Timothy O'Leary, and Jana Sawicki, (Malden Mass.: Wiley-Blackwell), 11-83.

2   The translated titles of Foucault's works are not always direct translations of the original titles in French. *Folie et Déraison, for instance was* translated as *Madness and Civilization* in 1964, and *History of Madness* in 2006. For clarity both French and English titles will be given throughout where any confusion or ambiguity might be caused. For the complete English translation see of *Folie et Déraison* see Michel Foucault, *History of Madness*, ed. Jean Khalfa, trans. Jonathan Murphy (London: Routledge, 2006).

3   Michel Foucault, *Birth of the Clinic: An Archaeology of Medical Perception*, trans. A.M. Sheridan Smith (London: Tavistock, 1973).

4   Michel Foucault, *The Order of Things: An Archaeology of the Human Sciences, trans.* Anonymous (London: Tavistock, 1970).

5   Michel Foucault, *The Archaeology of Knowledge and the Discourse on Language*, trans. A.M. Sheridan Smith and Rupert Swyer (London: Tavistock, 1972).

6   Michel Foucault, *Discipline and Punish: The Birth of the Prison, trans. A.M Sheridan Smith (London: Allen Lane, 1977).*

7   Michel Foucault, *The History of Sexuality,* 3 vols., trans. Robert Hurley, (New York: Pantheon, 1978-86).

8   On Foucault and the PCF in general, see James Miller, *The Passion of Michel Foucault* (New York: Simon & Schuster, 1993), 57-59.

MODULE 2
ACADEMIC CONTEXT

KEY POINTS

- Though Foucault's work as a whole does not fit neatly into a single field, "What is an Author?" is generally classed as literary theory.

- In the 1960s, France was home to many theorists who worked mainly across literature, history, and philosophy.

- Foucault was closely and personally involved with the "French theory"* scene and its ongoing debates.

The Work in its Context

Michel Foucault's "What is an Author?" is a work of literary and historical theory. It is the product of a time in French thought that has come to be seen as a watershed in intellectual history. The 1960s is the decade when "theory," or "French theory" as it is often called, was born.

This label is retrospective but nevertheless useful for describing both Foucault's own work (otherwise commonly deemed unclassifiable) and the context it came from.[1] Interdisciplinary, and therefore difficult to describe without oversimplification, "theory" was born from thinkers working across literature, philosophy, and history to critically analyze the accepted truths of their disciplines. Incorporating insights from political theory, psychology, and linguistics, many of the French theorists (including Foucault) worked through skeptical "archaeologies" or "genealogies" of ideas long taken for granted by society at large.

Though frequently in vigorous debate with each other, these theorists participated in what was in some sense a common project. By

66 shortly before his death [...] Foucault chose to describe his work as a whole as constituting a 'critical history of thought.' At other times Foucault described his work, in a related manner, as constituting a 'history of the present' 99

Barry Smart, *Foucault*

showing that such ideas had shifted and changed throughout history, the French theorists often made it impossible to take them for granted or see them as natural any longer. Foucault's immediate environment included major figures such as Jacques Derrida,* Gilles Deleuze,* and Julia Kristeva.* With regard to "What is an Author?" specifically, however, the work of Louis Althusser* and Roland Barthes is particularly relevant.

Overview of the Field

The two most important theoretical contexts for "What is an Author?" are Marxism* and structuralism.* These two schools of thought, often in dialogue, deeply informed Foucault's approach to texts in the essay.

Marxism was important both to the general French intellectual tradition in Foucault's time and to his education in particular. Based on the thought of nineteenth century German philosopher and economist Karl Marx, Marxism comes in many varieties. Along with providing the theoretical basis for Communism,* Marxism provided scholars with powerful tools for conceptualizing the relationship between texts, their creators, and their historical contexts.[2] Importantly for Foucault's work, a crucial tenet of Marxism is that human nature has changed across the course of history, and that individuals' "subjectivity"—a technical term for "personhood"—is created by the economic conditions of their society. Expanded and diversified by thinkers familiar to Foucault—especially Louis Althusser—Marxist* thought was heavily influential for scholars seeking to relate texts to their historical contexts.

The second school of thought to inform literary theory in Foucault's academic context was structuralism. A similarly varied movement, famous for its complexity, structuralism originated with Swiss linguist Ferdinand de Saussure,* before being exported to other academic contexts by French anthropologist Claude Levi-Strauss.* At its most basic, structuralism argues that the meanings of cultural phenomena stem from their relationships to each other and to larger systems or structures. For example, in order to understand a text readers work via an often unconscious knowledge of the structures within which it works, such as genre or narrative form. Without knowledge of those structures, the meaning of the text cannot be discerned.[3]

Alongside Marxism, structuralism was the dominant intellectual movement in 1950s and 1960s France. Foucault's 1966 book *Les mots et les choses* (translated as *The Order of Things*) is "Recognizably a structuralist history" for its attention to the structures that generate "knowledge" in history.[4] This thread continues with "What is an Author?" and one structuralist figure above all is crucial for understanding the essay: Foucault's friend Roland Barthes.

Academic Influences

Though Foucault was never an orthodox Marxist, he was both familiar with and influenced by the movement. This was, above all, due to his long intellectual and academic relationship with Louis Althusser. The leading French Marxist theoretician of the time (though not widely published or known until the mid 1960s), Althusser taught philosophy at the École Normale Supérieure from 1948. It was Althusser who encouraged Foucault to join the French Communist Party (PCF) in

1950, and who helped form Foucault's approach to the relationship between individuals and power in society.[5]

Althusser's work explores the ways in which "Ideological State Apparatuses"* (e.g. schools, prisons, and police) "administer" people's subjectivity. Althusser used the term both in the standard sense of bureaucratic administration, and in the expanded sense of "administering" something like medicine. He argued that states shape the kind of citizens they require by regulating the formation of their personhood from birth.[6] Often described as a "structural Marxist" for situating the subjectivity of individuals in a web of structural relationships, Althusser deeply affected Foucault's interest in mental health institutions and prisons.[7] This same influence can be traced in the concern of "What is an Author?" with the legal status of authorship.

Roland Barthes had an even more direct impact on Foucault's approach to literature. Eleven years Foucault's senior, Barthes gained fame in the 1950s for his masterful dissections of hidden meanings in a wide variety of cultural phenomena—from adverts to the Eiffel Tower—in magazine articles subsequently collected as *Mythologies* (1957). To Barthes, the task of structuralism was less to discover meaning than, as Josué Harari* puts it, to find "the rules governing the production of meaning."[8] In Barthes' own words, structuralism asks "how meaning is possible," a task shared to some extent by "What is an Author?"[9]

From 1956 onward, Barthes and Foucault were close friends. The two of them went on holiday together and frequently met for dinner in Paris. "What is an Author?" which was a direct response to Barthes' most famous and most controversial essay "The Death of the Author," is just one part of an ongoing public and private dialogue between the two men.

NOTES

1   See, e.g., Vincent B. Leitch ed., *The Norton Anthology of Theory and Criticism,* 2nd ed. (New York ; London: W. W. Norton, 2010), 1469.

2   For an introductory discussion of Marx's contribution to literary and cultural theory, see Gavin Grindon and Michael Ryan, "Marxism" in *The Encyclopedia of Literary and Cultural Theory*, eds. Gregory Castle, Robert Eaglestone, and M. Keith Booker (Chichester: Wiley-Blackwell, 2011), 312ff.

3   For an extended discussion of main currents in structuralism, see Jack Solomon, "Structuralism" in *The Encyclopedia of Literary and Cultural Theory*, eds. Gregory Castle, Robert Eaglestone, and M. Keith Booker Booker (Chichester: Wiley-Blackwell, 2011), 437ff.

4   *Norton Anthology*, 1469. On the complex relationship between *Les Mots et les Choses* and structuralism, however, see David Macey, *The Lives of Michel Foucault* (London: Hitchinson, 1993), 72-74.

5   See Macey, *Lives of Michel Foucault*, pp.29-30 and James Miller, *The Passion of Michel Foucault* (New York: Simon & Schuster, 1993), 57-59.

6   For a representative selection of texts outlining Althusser's theories, see *Norton Anthology*, 1332-1361.

7   See, e.g., Gavin Grindon and Michael Ryan, "Marxism" in *The Encyclopedia of Literary and Cultural Theory*, eds. Gregory Castle, Robert Eaglestone, and M. Keith Booker (Chichester: Wiley-Blackwell, 2011), 696.

8   Josué V. Harari, "Critical Factions/Critical Fictions" in *Textual Strategies: Perspectives in Post-Structuralist Criticism*, ed. Josué V. Harari (Ithaca: Cornell University Press, 1979), 22.

9   Roland Barthes, *Critical Essays*, trans. Richard Howard (Evanston: Northwestern University Press, 1972), 218.

MODULE 3
THE PROBLEM

KEY POINTS

- The place of the author in assessing or deducing a text's meaning is a central issue in traditional literary criticism.

- The debate centered on whether the author's intention creates the meaning of a text or if it is created by the reader's response.

- Foucault shifted the debate to ask what precisely is meant by the term "author" and how that relates to the meanings and functions of texts in society.

Core Question

Michel Foucault's 1969 "What is an Author?" addresses the complex issue of the relationship between authorial intention and the meaning of texts. As French literary theorist Antoine Compagnon* notes, the place of the author is one of the most "stormy" debates in literary theory.[1] The debate comes back to a fundamental question: what defines or generates a text's meaning?

Compagnon outlines three camps of critics who address this. The first camp belongs to the oldest tradition of "common sense" literary criticism. Here, it was generally accepted that the meaning of a text is the meaning *the author intended to put into it*. Understanding a text, in this tradition, means finding out what the author wants to communicate. Thus, the critic's job is either to find out directly what an author intended to say (e.g. from their letters or diaries) or to do so by processes of deduction.[2]

This approach came under attack by several groups of theorists during the twentieth century. Together they comprise Compagnon's

> **" The most controversial point in literary studies is the place of the author. "**
>
> Antoine Compagnon, *Le Démon de la théorie*

second camp. These included the Russian Formalists* (prominent around the 1910s to the1930s), the Anglo-American New Critics* (prominent in the 1940s and 1950s), and the French Structuralists* (prominent in the 1950s and 1960s). In different ways, these theorists advocated looking for a text's significance regardless of authorial intention.

Compagnon's third camp, just emerging around the time of Foucault's essay, put emphasis instead on reader reception. They suggested, to varying extents, that meaning was generated primarily by reader interactions with texts.

To Compagnon's trio we can add a fourth camp also emerging around this time: critics, often influenced by Marxist theory, seeking to root texts in historical, social, and intellectual contexts. To varying degrees, these historicist* critics also demoted authorial intention as a priority. They analyzed texts as products of particular social and economic conditions rather than as products of individual authors.

The Participants

Debates around authorial intention were not limited to France. In 1946, the American New Critics William K. Wimsatt Jr. and Monroe C. Beardsley published their famous paper "The Intentional Fallacy." This targeted the common assumption that authorial intention defined the true meaning of texts. The New Critics insisted instead that meaning inheres in texts as aesthetic objects. A poem, for instance, may generate effects and meanings beyond or even contradictory to its author's intention, and, accordingly, it should be judged and understood by these. Above all, Wimsatt and Beardsley argued that part of the problem is that we cannot *know* an author's intention. Therefore, the "intention of the author is neither available nor desirable as a standard for judging the success of a work of literary art."[3]

The French debate, though separate, occurred along similar lines: traditionalist advocates of author–centered criticism versus the predominantly structuralist proponents of *nouvelle critique*.*[4] Foremost among the structuralists was Roland Barthes, who, across a series of books and articles from 1963 to 1968, entered into a savage debate with the traditionalist Raymond Picard.* The debate culminated in Barthes's famous 1968 essay "The Death of the Author," which directly stimulated Foucault's essay.

The Contemporary Debate

The Barthes-Picard debate demonstrates two poles of the argument around the author. Barthes's 1963 book *On Racine* examined the works of seventeenth century French playwright Jean Racine* to discern a single "deep unifying structure." Intended as a critique of what Barthes called "university criticism," *On Racine* still aimed partially at an authorial "deep consciousness or intentionality," but decidedly not in the traditional manner.[5]

On Racine provoked a strong reaction from Picard, who was both a leading university professor and a Racine specialist. In 1965's *Nouvelle critique ou Nouvelle Imposture (New Criticism, or New Fraud?)* he accused Barthes of combining a dogmatic and jargon–filled interpretative framework with analysis that was both arbitrary and subjective.[6] Most of all, Picard defended the idea that literary criticism could and should be objective. Picard pointed to "the deliberate and lucid intention that gave birth to [the text]" as a central truth that criticism sought, objectively, to discover.[7]

Barthes retrenched his position with *Criticism and Truth* (1965), making two central arguments. First: writers' intentions are not psychologically pure or lucidly willed. In other words, the writer often does not know what they intend in a text. Even if they did, language is a problematic tool for translating such intentions. "A writer," Barthes argues, "is someone for whom language constitutes a problem."[8] Second: language cannot be simply tied to its origins; words develop new meanings over time, and these too are part of a text's significance. Thus, instead of giving or rediscovering a text's supposed meaning, the critic should describe the logic by which "meanings are engendered in a manner capable of being *accepted*" by readers.[9] In other words, the critic's task is to discern the shared structures that allow meaning to be both produced and understood. In this light, Barthes continues, "Criticism is not science. Science deals with meanings, criticism produces them."[10]

Barthes took a more extreme stance in his most famous essay, "The Death of the Author" (1968). This essay refuted the idea that a text contained "the 'message' of the Author-God." Instead, it argued that a text is "a multi-dimensional space in which a variety of writings, none of them original, blend and clash [...] a tissue of quotations."[11] The author is now not an author at all but a "scriptor": a vehicle for inscribing these quotations. Meaning, meanwhile, does not come from the scriptor, but begins with the reader. With this in mind, Barthes pronounced that it was time for a new mode of critical reading: "to give writing its future, it is necessary to overthrow the myth [of the author]: the birth of the reader must be at the cost of the death of the Author."[12]

NOTES

1   Antoine Compagnon, *Le Démon de la théorie: Littérature et sens commun* (Paris: Seuil, 1998), 51 (my translation).

2   Compagnon, *Démon*, 51.

3   See William K. Wimsatt Jr. and Monroe C. Beardsley, "The Intentional Fallacy", in *The Norton Anthology of Theory and Criticism / Vincent B. Leitch, General Editor*, 2nd ed., ed. Vincent B. Leitch (New York ; London: W. W. Norton, 2010), 1233.

4   *Nouvelle critique* also means "new criticism", but should not confused with the American New Criticism. As a contemporary French critic noted, many of the ideas promoted by *la nouvelle critique* were already current in both Russian and Anglo-American literary theory, but it remained a separate movement. See R. Fayolle, "Review: *Nouvelle critique ou nouvelle imposture*, by Raymond Picard", in *Revue d'Histoire Littéraire de la France 67*, no. 1 (1967), 175.

5   Compagnon, *Démon*, 75.

6   Raymond Picard, *Nouvelle critique ou Nouvelle Imposture* (Paris, Pauvert, 1965)

7   See Raymond Picard, *Nouvelle critique,* 121-123, and Compagnon, *Démon*, 74-76.

8   Roland Barthes, *Criticism and Truth, ed. and trans. Katrine Pilcher Keuneman* (London: Continuum, 2007), 23-24.

9   Barthes, *Criticism and Truth*, 31.

10 Barthes, *Criticism and Truth*, 32.

11 Roland Barthes, "The Death of the Author", in *The Norton Anthology of Theory and Criticism / Vincent B. Leitch, General Editor*, 2nd ed., ed. Vincent B. Leitch (New York ; London: W. W. Norton, 2010), 1324.

12 Barthes, "Death of the Author," 1326.

MODULE 4
THE AUTHOR'S CONTRIBUTION

KEY POINTS

- Foucault's response to the debate on authorial intention was to ask what we mean by "author," and examine "the author" across history.

- Examining the historical meanings of "author" allowed Foucault to escape circular debates around intention and meaning.

- Foucault's approach was closely related to his own work on discourse and power.

Author's Aims

Michel Foucault's "What is an Author?" turns the debates around authorial intention and the "death of the author" on their heads to attack them from a different angle. But, as Foucault explained to the essay's original audience in 1969, he is himself "far from offering a solution" to the problems surrounding the author.[1] Instead, it is his intention to raise and highlight the questions posed by the figure of the author.

Foucault outlined four areas in which he wanted to interrogate the idea of the author:[2]

- To ask what we mean by "the name of the author," since authors' names work in some way differently to people's names in the general sense.
- To consider how "appropriation" works regarding authors and texts, since "the author is neither exactly the owner nor the person in charge of his texts; and nor is he the producer or the inventor of them."
- To consider how attribution works by asking what it means to

> ❝ It is not enough [...] to repeat the empty affirmation that the author has disappeared. ❞
>
> Michel Foucault, "What is an Author?"

attribute or de-attribute a text to an author, and questioning how we do this.

- To consider "the position of the author" regarding a text. In everyday speech, the meaning of words like "I," "you," or "today" is clear, but in authored texts their meaning is unclear. "I," for instance, very rarely means "I the author;" so what does it mean exactly? How does the author's position in and/ or outside of the text change, depending on the type of text involved?

These are four complex areas, and though Foucault regarded Roland Barthes's "death of the author" thesis as a dead end, he makes clear that he sees his own essay as an unfinished, open-ended response to it. His central aim was to shift the debate from the sterile opposition between Barthes and more traditional literary critics like Raymond Picard. This is an aim that "What is an Author?" fulfills entirely.

Approach

Two central constants in Foucault's entire body of work are key to understanding "What is an Author?" The first is the examination of theoretical or philosophical questions through historical specifics. The second is the examination of how individuals, language, and discourse are shaped by power relations in society.

In contrast to Roland Barthes's desire to theorize around authorship away from its many historical incarnations, "What is an Author?" attempts to theorize on the basis of historical evidence. As Foucault points out, authorship "does not affect all discourses in the same way at all times and in all types of civilization."[3] He is interested in the different forms the author has taken throughout history, and how this has affected the relationship of authors to the meaning of their texts.

This is directly linked to Foucault's interest in power through the essay's discussion of the legal status of authors. As Foucault notes, the idea of the author "is linked to the juridical and institutional system" of the society in which the author lives.[4] Laws, he argues, are what tie authors to texts, by giving them both ownership and responsibility for what they say. In other words, authorship becomes important when authorities want to be able to punish people for the texts they produce. For example, if those texts are regarded as transgressive due to reasons of political dissent, or religious or sexual obscenity.

The focus on the idea of the author within history as defined by power structures in society marks a decisive original turn in the debates around authorial intention. It marked Foucault out both from traditional literary critics' reliance on biographical detail, and from Barthes's radical move of placing authors aside in favor of readers.

Contribution in Context

"What is an Author?" is indebted to Foucault's direct intellectual environment. As a response to Barthes's "The Death of the Author," the essay is defined by opposition to non-historicist ideas of authorship. It should, though, be seen as influenced by both Barthes and his opponents. "What is an Author?" works partially from the traditionalist stance that the author cannot be ignored, while accepting Barthes's contention that interpretation cannot be settled by falling back on authorial intention.

Foucault's historicist approach, meanwhile, is owed to his own work and intellectual background. As noted above, his interest in the relationship between individuals, power, and society has its roots in Marxist thought, and owes its development to his former tutor,

Marxist philosopher Louis Althusser. It was Foucault himself who took the examination of social and intellectual history through power dynamics to new levels. This approach is now inextricably linked to Foucault's name.

In this sense, "What is an Author?" owes its existence above all to developments in Foucault's own thinking. Though it remains a small-scale outline of possibilities rather than a complete project, the essay fits in with the more ambitious projects of *Les mots et les choses* and *L'Archéologie du savoir.* Both of these works examine the ways in which human discourses—from individual texts to larger structures of knowledge—have changed through history in relation to the changing structures and institutions of society. Though he does not use the word in the essay, "What is an Author?" can justifiably be described as an archaeology of authorship.

NOTES

1   Michel Foucault, *Dits et Écrits*, eds. Daniel Defert and François Ewald (Paris: Gallimard, 1994), vol. 1, 789 (my translation).

2   All quotations in the following points are from Foucault, *Dits et Écrits*, vol. 1, 789-790 (my translation).

3   Michel Foucault, "What is an Author?", in *The Essential Works of Michel Foucault, 1954-1984. Vol. 2, Aesthetics*, ed. Paul Rabinow (London: Penguin, 2000), 216.

4   Foucault, "What is an Author?", 216.

SECTION 2
IDEAS

MAIN IDEAS

KEY POINTS

- Foucault argues that contemporary debates over authorship missed the real relationships between authors, texts, and their meanings.

- Foucault's central argument is that critics should investigate not individual authors, but what he terms "the author function."

- Foucault's argument is targeted at an audience of specialists and can present a challenge to students and non-specialists.

Key Themes

Michel Foucault's 1969 essay "What is an Author?" focuses on opening new avenues of enquiry about authors and the meanings of their texts. Its overarching argument is that we can neither treat the author of a text as a real person (whose intentions we can know, and whose intentions explain the work) nor as an absence or dead figure (who has no impact on or control over the meaning of the work).

Foucault argues that neither of these approaches reveals much of real significance about a text or about the society that produced it. As a social activist, philosopher, and historian of ideas, Foucault is interested in precisely the latter, so he suggests a third approach. Taking a question from Samuel Beckett* as his starting point, Foucault asks "What does it matter who is speaking?" in or through a text. Unlike Barthes, he suggests that it does on some level matter "who is speaking," but it matters primarily in relation to the specific social processes at specific points in history. Instead of examining authors as individuals, therefore,

> " 'What does it matter who is speaking,' someone said,
> 'what does it matter who is speaking.' "
>
> Samuel Beckett, *Texts for Nothing*, "Text 3"

we should look at the idea of the "author function" and how it relates to certain kinds of texts in certain kinds of society.

The specifics of the "author function" and how it relates to different kinds of discourse (Foucault's term for texts, kinds of texts, and particular ways of using language to express knowledge of the world) will be discussed below. For the moment, however, it is worth noting that despite the seemingly fine distinction between "author" and "author function," the shift leads to a radical conclusion. As Foucault explains, it means that we must "entirely reverse the traditional idea of the author."[1] Instead of seeing him or her as "the genial creator of a work" to which he or she gives "an inexhaustible variety of significations," we should see him or her as "a certain functional principle" by which "one limits, excludes, and chooses" significations.[2] In other words, rather than opening up a world of possible meanings, "the author" is a construct that curtails and limits possible meanings.

Exploring the Ideas

It is key to Foucault's argument that the author cannot be treated as a "real person." Among other reasons, this is because an author's name is complex, with different meanings and different ways of being affected by reality. A real person's name, like "Pierre Dupont," does not tell us anything about him. But an author's name does. "Shakespeare"* is "the equivalent of a description" or series of descriptions.[3] The name "Shakespeare" does not just designate a person, it also *means* several things: the man who wrote *Hamlet*,* the national poet of England, and so on.[4]

Because of this, authors' names can be affected by certain kinds of shifts in our knowledge. If "we proved that Shakespeare did not write those sonnets which pass for his," or that he did produce other famous works now known by other authors' names, "that would entirely modify the functioning of his name."[5] Similarly, if we said "Pierre Dupont does not exist," that is "not at all the same thing as saying that Homer* […] did not exist."[6] In reality, Homer probably did not exist as a lone author who wrote the *Odyssey** and the *Iliad*,* but the name "Homer" still has a status and a set of functions as an author.

Crucially, the author's name is really a *function*: it "performs a certain role," or set of roles.[7] It groups texts together, defines and contrasts them to others, and allows us to treat them in certain ways. Most of all, it "serves to characterize a certain mode of being of discourse." [8] If "one can say 'this was written by so-and-so' or 'so-and-so is its author,'" we know that "this discourse is not everyday speech that merely comes and goes." Instead, it "must be received in a certain mode and […], in a given culture, must receive a certain status."[9]

In our culture, Foucault asserts, the author function has four characteristics:

1. It is linked to the legal system through both ownership rights (i.e. copyright laws) and the state's desire to be able to punish the originators of transgressive works.
2. It does not affect "all discourses in a universal and constant way."[10] For example, historically, literary texts have often circulated anonymously, while "scientific" texts were once only respected if they came from a recognized authority (such as Aristotle* or Galen*); now the situation is largely reversed.
3. The author function "does not develop spontaneously" but appears as the "result of a complex operation that constructs a

certain being of reason that we call the 'author.'"[11] This depends very much on what we accept as being the author's work (or not), and on how we define "work." For example, do letters, shopping lists, etc. by authors count?

4. Finally, the author function is not "a pure and simple reconstruction made secondhand from a text," but something more complicated. It is related to a real-life person—the author—but cannot be equated with him or her. Instead "the author function is carried out and operates in the scission [...] this division and this distance" between the "author," "the real writer," and "the fictitious speaker."[12] In other words, it is created by and exists in the gap between our idea of the author, the real-life writer, and the voice of the text itself.

Foucault suggests that we must attend to these four problematics if we are to go beyond the old debates on authorial intention.

Language and Expression

Though it requires patience and concentration "What is an Author?" is a readable and engaging work. It can, though, be challenging for students. The essay's central difficulty lies in its use of specialized technical vocabulary and terminology. Originally delivered as a lecture to specialists, it was written with the assumption that the audience is familiar with the main lines of the debate on authorial intention and the specialist vocabulary Foucault uses.

In terms of specialist vocabulary, the most challenging term, "discourse," is key in Foucault's work as a whole. In practice, "discourse" can have meanings which range from the highly specific to the entirely generalized. A discourse might be simply an instance of speech or text, or it might be an entire subset of language use with specific properties (i.e. scientific discourse, literary discourse, legal discourse). Perhaps most importantly, it can also refer to the whole set of practices and languages by which society replicates its knowledge, behavior, and values. This is why, for Foucault, power and discourse go hand in hand. This idea is vital for a clear understanding of "What is an Author?"[13]

NOTES

1   Michel Foucault, "What is an Author?", in *The Essential Works of Michel Foucault, 1954-1984. Vol. 2, Aesthetics*, ed. Paul Rabinow (London: Penguin, 2000), 221.

2   Foucault, "What is an Author?", 221.

3   Foucault, "What is an Author?", 209.

4   Foucault, "What is an Author?", 209.

5   Foucault, "What is an Author?", 210.

6   Foucault, "What is an Author?", 210.

7   Foucault, "What is an Author?", 211.

8   Foucault, "What is an Author?", 211.

9   Foucault, "What is an Author?", 211.

10 Foucault, "What is an Author?", 212.

11 Foucault, "What is an Author?", 213.

12 Foucault, "What is an Author?", 215.

13 For a fuller discussion of "discourse" as a theoretical term, see Yasser Munif, "Discourse" in Gregory Castle, Robert Eaglestone, and M. Keith Booker eds., *The Encyclopedia of Literary and Cultural Theory* (Chichester: Wiley-Blackwell, 2011), and Sara Mills, *Discourse* (London: Routledge, 2004).

MODULE 6
SECONDARY IDEAS

KEY POINTS

- Foucault examines "authors" of theories or traditions, calls for a "typology of discourse," and considers the possible disappearance of the author.

- These secondary ideas have had less impact and influence than the central argument, but remain important in context.

- Foucault's secondary ideas have inspired discourse studies and have proven applicable to cultural theory in the age of the internet.

Other Ideas

Michel Foucault's 1969 essay "What is an Author?" holds three secondary ideas of interest to students and critics. All three are part of Foucault's deliberately open-ended approach to his subject. Having identified the author function as imposing a limit on interpretation, Foucault himself is keen to remove such limits. He does so at the end of the essay by proposing three new directions.

The first concerns Foucault's sense that it was intellectually unjustifiable to limit himself to a purely text-centered idea of authorship. Put simply, he asks what other kinds of objects or discourses can be authored. As he points out, Sigmund Freud* was in some way the "author" of psychoanalysis,* though it is an ongoing discourse in which many other authors have participated. This relates to authorship in a way that Foucault suggests requires further investigation. How, he asks, might "authored discourses" of this kind reflect on the idea of the author function?

> **❝ I have unjustifiably limited my subject. ❞**
> Michel Foucault, "What is an Author?"

The second secondary idea is Foucault's call for the author function to be incorporated into a "historical analysis of discourse."[1] What can the author function tell us about how discourses have circulated in societies through history? And what can that tell us about our own society?

The third secondary idea is what one theorist has called Foucault's "maddeningly brief" look at the possibility that the author function will disappear from our culture.[2] What if, Foucault asks, the conditions of discourse change in such a way that authors no longer impede the totally free circulation of texts. What if, to return to the essay's opening question, it made no difference who was speaking?

Exploring the Ideas

As Foucault notes, "one can be the author of much more than a book."[3] Aside from music or fine art, one can author a theory, tradition, or discipline in which "other books and authors will in their turn find a place."[4] How, Foucault asks, do we approach a figure like Sigmund Freud who has, in some sense, authored an entire field?

Foucault's response is, in his own words, "very schematic;" he makes it clear that he is raising the subject predominantly to show the complexity of the author function.[5] It is, he notes, "complex enough when one tries to situate it at the level of a book or a series of texts," but it "involves still more determining factors when one tries to analyze it in larger units;" this is a problem he sets aside for another time.[6]

Complexity also lies behind the second secondary idea, which is perhaps the crux of the essay. As the author function is so complex and so deeply related to certain kinds of discourse, Foucault calls for a deeper study of it as a means of performing a "historical analysis of discourse."[7] As noted above, he is interested in literature not primarily for itself, but as a means of understanding the history of ideas and society. As discourse is, for Foucault, the most significant structuring aspect of society, it is natural for him to question whether the insight of the author function has wider implications.

For Foucault, these ideas are inevitably bound up with power, which is inextricably related to how discourses circulate in society. It is significant that the author function has so much to do with legal power, for text-producers over their own texts, and for states over texts and text-producers both. In other words, copyright gives writers legal ownership of their texts, which allows them to control circulation and make money from their work. But, at the same time, it also allows states to hold writers responsible and punish them if their work is deemed transgressive or dangerous. Similarly, the author function serves to limit readers' interpretations: the "author" becomes a figure for ruling out interpretations he or she cannot have intended, thereby preventing texts from being interpreted too freely. Thus, for Foucault, the author is not the source of meaning but "the ideological figure by which one marks the manner in which we fear the proliferation of meaning."[8]

This is the source of his final idea in the essay. While it would be "pure romanticism" to imagine a society in which neither authors nor such fears existed, he takes a moment to consider the possibility.[9] It would be a world in which "All discourses, whatever their status, form, value, and whatever the treatment to which they will be subjected, would develop in the anonymity of a murmur."[10] With this, the old questions—"Who really spoke? Is it really he and not someone else? With what authenticity or originality?"—would disappear.[11] Instead, critics and theorists would ask questions relating to discourse and power, indifferent to the old question of who is speaking.[12]

Overlooked

"What is an Author?" has a paradoxical status in terms of overlooked ideas. Depending on what group of readers is being talked about, it is simultaneously a text that has attracted a great deal of attention, and very little.

On one hand, Foucault scholars justifiably regard "What is an Author?" as only a minor text in his body of work. This fact is marked out by the essay's relative absence from guides dedicated to Foucault's career as a whole.[13] In Foucault studies, attention to similar themes tends to focus instead on *The Archaeology of Knowledge*, which appeared in the same year and delves far more deeply into the history and typology of discourses. At the same time, however, "What is an Author?" does mark, as Simon During has noted, an important staging post in Foucault's thought during the late 1960s, and should be read as such.[14]

Simultaneously, literary critics and students who tend to read "What is an Author?" out of context have consistently treated it as more literary and more central to Foucault's thought than it in fact is. The historian of French theory François Cusset* notes that this is a general trend in American reception of French theorists—who were for the most part not primarily literary academics—but that Foucault is perhaps the most extreme example. This, he notes, is due in part to the wide circulation of "What is an Author?" in the United States from 1979 onward.[15] As such, it is standard for literary specialists to overlook the fact that, with its interest in discourse as a general category, "What is an Author?" is in fact "resolutely anti-literary."[16]

NOTES

1   Michel Foucault, "What is an Author?", in *The Essential Works of Michel Foucault, 1954-1984. Vol. 2, Aesthetics*, ed. Paul Rabinow (London: Penguin, 2000), 220.

2   Mark Poster, "The Digital Subject and Cultural Theory", in *The Book History Reader*, 2nd ed., eds. David Finkelstein and Alistair McCleery (London: Routledge, 2006), 489.

3   Foucault, "What is an Author?", 217.

4   Foucault, "What is an Author?", 217.

5   Foucault, "What is an Author?", 220.

6   Foucault, "What is an Author?", 220.

7   Foucault, "What is an Author?", 220.

8   Foucault, "What is an Author?", 220.

9   Foucault, "What is an Author?", 222.

10 Foucault, "What is an Author?", 222.

11 Foucault, "What is an Author?", 222.

12 Foucault, "What is an Author?", 222.

13 See, for example, the lack of sustained attention in either Gary Gutting ed., *The Cambridge Companion to Foucault*, 2nd edition (Cambridge: Cambridge University Press, 2005), or any critical attention at all in Christopher Falzon, Timothy O'Leary, and Jana Sawicki eds., *A Companion to Foucault* (Malden Mass.: Wiley-Blackwell, 2013). The essay's reception, as part of Foucault's general impact on literary theory, is, though, usefully discussed in Lisa Downing, *The Cambridge Introduction to Foucault* (Cambridge: Cambridge University Press, 2008), 53-68. The same pattern is, not coincidentally, also seen in the reception of Roland Barthes' "The Death of the Author", as noted by John Logie, "1967: The Birth of the 'The Death of the Author'", *College English*, Vo. 75, No. 5 (May 2013), 496.

14 Simon During, *Foucault and Literature: Towards a Genealogy of Writing* (London: Routledge), 118.

15 See François Cusset, *French Theory: How Foucault, Derrida, Deleuze, & Co. Transformed the Intellectual Life of the United States*, trans. Jeff Fort, Josephine Berganza and Marlon Jones (Mineapolis: University of Minnesota Press, 2008), 79.

16 During, *Foucault and Literature,* 122.

MODULE 7
ACHIEVEMENT

KEY POINTS

- "What is an Author?" succeeds on its own terms and remains a seminal theoretical text in literary studies.

- One of the most significant factors in the essay's success was its circulation in the United States.

- Despite its seminal status, "What is an Author?" remains a sketchy and suggestive fragment of a project left unfulfilled.

Assessing the Argument

To give a fair assessment of "What is an Author?" it is useful to remember the essay's original context, including Michel Foucault's prefatory remarks and the debate he had with his listeners. These are only available in the transcript of Foucault's original lecture, published in the *Bulletin de la Société française de philosophie* in 1969.[1] Here Foucault is clear that he was presenting an unfinished work. As he put it in the post-lecture debate, he had sketched his thoughts "very roughly" (*très grossièrement*), and in a deliberately "abstract" way as a means of "laying out his stall" (*une mise en place d'ensemble*). It was, he goes on to suggest, more a "survey of the building site" than an attempt to build.[2]

Given that Foucault's audience on this occasion included major intellectual figures such as Jacques Lacan* and Lucien Goldmann,* it is easy to perceive a mixture of rhetorical modesty and defensiveness in these remarks. But, at the same time, they indicate that "What is an Author?" should be regarded as laying out possibilities and opening up questions rather than staking out a firm position. As Adrian Wilson has noted, Foucault's primary aims were to respond to Roland Barthes's

> 66 Unfortunately what I am presenting today is far too thin to merit your attention; it is [...] an attempt at an analysis whose main lines I can as yet barely make out 99
>
> Michel Foucault "What is an Author?"

"The Death of the Author," and "to problematize" the figure of the author.[3] It is, therefore, a text characterized by uncertainties rather than conclusions.

On these terms, however, Foucault presents an undeniably strong argument. Though he does not go deeply into historical specifics, Foucault forms a convincing argument for using the author function as a means of conceptualizing the complex way in which writers, readers, and texts interact. He does so by appealing to the different manifestations of authority and anonymity across history, and to how legal frameworks have fixed the concept of authorship in new ways, particularly from the eighteenth century onward.[4]

Achievement in Context

The achievement of "What is an Author?" can be summed up in a single sentence. As Adrian Wilson puts it, it made clear how "the figure of the 'author' is an interpretative construct: a construct associated with canonical words, notionally identified as the writer of such works, but none the less categorically distinct from that writer."[5] In other words, Foucault made it possible to see how the "author" and the real person who wrote a given text are not the same thing. The "author" is meant to be precisely that, but is not. Instead, he or she is a tool built to aid and ground interpretations of the text. A markedly less extreme stance than Roland Barthes's famous "Death of the Author" polemic, this argument has met widespread acceptance in modern literary criticism, even when skeptically readdressed by critics.

The essay's impact was smaller in France than in the United States, but was notable nevertheless. Soon after its appearance, it exerted an influence on Roland Barthes's own thought concerning authorship. As Wilson notes, Barthes responded directly to the prominence that Foucault gave "the text" over "the work" in his own 1971 essay "From Work to Text."[6]

This swift response from Barthes neatly marks out Foucault's other main achievement with the essay. "What is an Author?" played a significant role in shifting emphasis from writers to the text itself. This is a shift in literary theory that gained momentum during the 1970s and 1980s, and has remained strong ever since.[7] In the United States, this can be traced directly to the important place of "What is an Author?" in the general uptake of "French theory" in North American universities from the 1970s onward.[8] It was one of the earliest works to be canonized as "French theory" after Foucault presented it, in a lightly modified version, at the University of Buffalo New York in 1970. First published in English in 1979, as part of a collection of short texts in literary theory, *Textual Strategies: Perspectives in Post-Structuralist* Literary Criticism*, it has had a central place in literary theory and on student reading lists ever since.[9]

Limitations

For a piece explicitly presented as a sketch or outline of possibilities, "What is an Author?" has gone on to have a remarkable afterlife. Indeed, it is partially thanks to its inconclusiveness that it has in many ways superseded the limitations Foucault was keen to point out. Despite originally being presented to an audience of specialized intellectuals, it has proven to be adaptable to a number of disciplines. Though a firm fixture on undergraduate literary theory courses across the world, "What is an Author?" can be found as part of history, sociology, law, and communication studies* courses, as well as in sub-disciplines such as book history* and the history of science.*

Speaking more generally, "What is an Author?" soon became a widely anthologized example of poststructuralist or postmodernist* theory. This put it both in the academic limelight, particularly from the 1980s onward, and in the firing line of harsh criticisms. Foucault, along with Roland Barthes, Jacques Derrida, and Jacques Lacan would eventually be accused of spreading, in the memorable phrase of one conservative critic, the "Gallic fog of deconstruction"* throughout literature departments across the world.[10]

NOTES

1   Michel Foucault, "Qu'est-ce qu'un auteur?", *Bulletin de la Société française de philosophie*, 63, no. 3, July-September 1969, pp.73-104. This is also the text reprinted in Michel Foucault, *Dits et Écrits*, eds. Daniel Defert and François Ewald (Paris: Gallimard, 1994). All citations below are to *Dits et Écrits*.

2   Foucault, *Dits et Écrits* 817.

3   Wilson, 343.

4   Foucault, *Dits et Écrits* 817.

5   Adrian Wilson, "Foucault on the 'Question of the Author': A Critical Exegesis", *The Modern Language Review*, Vol. 99, No. 2 (Apr., 2004), 360.

6   Wilson, "Foucault on the 'Question of the Author'", 343. For Barthes' essay, see Roland Barthes, "From Work to Text" in Vincent B. Leitch et al. eds., *The Norton Anthology of Theory and Criticism* (New York and London: W. W. Norton and Company, 2001), pp. 1326-1331.

7   See, on this point, Wilson, "Foucault on the 'Question of the Author'", 343.

8   See François Cusset, *French Theory: How Foucault, Derrida, Deleuze, & Co. Transformed the Intellectual Life of the United States*, trans. Jeff Fort, Josephine Berganza and Marlon Jones (Mineapolis: University of Minnesota Press, 2008), "Introduction", *passim*.

9   Josué V. Harari ed., *Textual Strategies: Perspectives in Post-Structuralist Criticism,* (Ithaca: Cornell University Press, 1979).

10 See Bruce Bawer, "The Case of Stephen Greenblatt" in *The New Criterion*, Vol. 36, No. 3 (November 2017), https://www.newcriterion.com/issues/2017/9/the-case-of-stephen-greenblatt-8753.

MODULE 8
PLACE IN THE AUTHOR'S WORK

KEY POINTS

- Foucault is an inter-disciplinary thinker whose work focused on analyzing how discourses and power structures confine individuals.

- Despite its significance for literary theory, "What is an Author?" is a minor piece in Foucault's overall project.

- "What is an Author?" helps introduce new readers to Foucault by providing a gateway to his major works.

Positioning

Despite its importance in literary theory, Michel Foucault's "What is an Author?" is undeniably a minor work in the overall context of his career—a career notable both for extreme productivity and astonishing variety. Foucault had already published five books by the time he presented "What is an Author?"[1] These included his seminal works *History of Madness*[2] and *Birth of the Clinic*,[3] as well as his equally seminal investigation into the history and sociology of the human sciences,* *Les mots et les choses* (translated in 1970 as *The Order of Things*).[4] When "What is an Author?" was presented in February 1969, Foucault was also extremely close to publishing yet another seminal text, *The Archaeology of Knowledge*, which appeared that March.[5]

Foucault's output of books slowed slightly after the 1960s, with his major book–length works from the 1970s limited to *Surveiller et punir* (1975; translated as *Discipline and Punish*),[6] and the incomplete, three-volume *History of Sexuality*.[7] Overall, though, he was as productive in other ways, with a steady flow of lectures, seminars, and interviews in

> **❝** I try to show, based upon their historical establishment, those systems which are still ours today and within which we are trapped. It is a question, basically, of presenting a critique of our own time, based upon retrospective analyses. **❞**
>
> Michel Foucault, *Partisan Review* Interview, 1971

both Europe and North America. His collected shorter works alone, *Dits et écrits, 1954-1988*—as yet untranslated into English—amount to four volumes in the original edition.[8]

It is notable that authorship is not a theme Foucault ever returned to explicitly, though he contributed to his "history of discourse" mentioned in "What is an Author?" with *The Archaeology of Knowledge*.[9] While he explicitly presented the lecture as an outline for further work, he never saw fit to substantially redraft or alter it for later audiences. When he presented "What is an Author?" again as a lecture in the United States in 1970, he made no substantial changes, and was happy for any of the three published versions available to be reprinted without making any distinction between them. It is clear that Foucault eventually came to see the essay as a standalone piece, which is how it has often been read by students of literature.

Integration

As a whole, Foucault's work is generally, and quite fairly, considered unclassifiable. Though much of it is historical in nature, it crosses disciplinary borders with ease. It is also marked by its use of material and theory from several disciplines—history, psychology, philosophy, sociology, and literary criticism—to serve its own ends. In terms of topics, his work ranges from psychology to the histories of science, medicine, punishment, and sexuality, among others. The literary is a recurring but only minor theme.[10]

Within such a vast output, it would be astonishing if a piece as short as "What is an Author?" played a major role, but it is nevertheless representative of certain fundamental themes in Foucault's work as a whole. With its interest in reconstructing a genealogy or archaeology of authorship, it is easy to see how it ties into the themes of both *Les mots et les choses* and *L'Archéologie du savoir*. As Simon During points out in *Foucault and Literature*, "What is an Author?" belongs far more alongside these books than any of Foucault's directly literary writings.[11] In looking toward discourse and governmentality,* the essay's concern with legal constructions and appropriations of the individual foreshadows *Surveiller et punir* and *The History of Sexuality*.

Through this, it is clear that "What is an Author?" is marked by something that Foucault considered representative of his work as a whole: a desire to "put 'in play,' show up, transform and reverse the systems which quietly order us about" in the things we take for granted. As Foucault pointed out in a 1971 interview, "As far as I am concerned, that is what I try to do in [all] my work."[12]

Significance

Foucault's reputation was already well established in France by the mid-1960s and burgeoned internationally at the turn of the 1970s. Only a year after presenting "What is an Author?" Foucault took up a position at the Collège de France—one of the highest accolades afforded by French academia. At the same time, he began to lecture by invitation in the United States, though his American lectures would only become a regular event later in the decade. Though "What is an Author?" was one of the first texts Foucault himself presented in the United States and it circulated widely, his early reputation there was based more on *The Order of Things,* which received a broadly favorable review from important literary critic George Steiner* in *The New York Times Book Review*.[13]

For all this, the "What is an Author?" essay was what might be termed a "sleeper hit" in the United States, thanks in no small part to its publication in Josué Harari's 1979 *Textual Strategies* series, which was one of the best-known introductions to French theory available at the time. In France, where it was not anthologized in the same way, "What is an Author?" largely sank without a trace. As Daniel Defert notes, despite the clear differences between Foucault's stance and those of his contemporaries Roland Barthes and Jacques Derrida, readers at the time took him to be saying the same things as them.[14]

Despite its minor status within Foucault's work as a whole, "What is an Author?" bears undeniable significance as one of his most accessible and most widely circulated theory texts in the English-speaking academic world. It remains, for many students, the ideal introduction both to a core issue in literary theory and to Foucault's thought.

NOTES

1   Foucault's bibliography is notoriously muddled by variant titles and variant versions of books in French, as well as by variant titles and versions in English. For a scholarly introduction to some of the issues see Richard A. Lynch, "Two Bibliographical Resources for Foucault's Work in English", *Foucault Studies*, No. 1, (December 2004), pp. 71-76. A useful, regularly updated annotated bibliography (including translations in several languages) can be accessed at https://monoskop.org/Michel_Foucault.

2   For a full English text including a brief history of the various versions available see Michel Foucault, *History of Madness*, ed. Jean Khalfa, trans. Jonathan Murphy (London: Routledge, 2006).

3   Michel Foucault, *Naissance de la Clinique: une archéologie du regard medical* (Paris: Presses Universitaires de France, 1963); Michel Foucault, *The Birth of the Clinic: An Archaeology of Medical Perception*, trans. A.M. Sheridan (London: Tavistock, 1973).

4   Michel Foucault *Les mots et les choses. Une archéologie des sciences humaines* (Paris: Gallimard, 1966; Michel Foucault, *The Order of Things*, trans. Anonymous (London: Tavistock, 1970).

5   Michel Foucault, *L'Archéologie du savoir*,(Paris: Gallimard,1969); Michel Foucault, *The Archaeology of Knowledge and the Discourse on Language*, trans. A. M. Sheridan Smith and Rupert Swyer (New York: Pantheon Books, 1972).

6   Michel Foucault, *Surveiller et punir: naissance de la prison* (Paris: Gallimard, 1975); Michel Foucault, *Discipline and Punish: The Birth of the Prison*, trans. A.M. Sheridan (London: Allen Lane, 1977).

7   Michel Foucault, *Histoire de la sexualité*, 3 vols (Paris: Gallimard, 1976-84); Michel Foucault, *The History of Sexuality*, 3 vols., trans. Robert Hurley (New York: Pantheon, 1978-86).

8   Michel Foucault, *Dits et écrits, 1954-1988*, 4 vols., eds. Daniel Defert and François Ewald (Paris: Gallimard, 1994).

9   For a clear and useful introduction to the stages and overall arc of Foucault's concerns across his career see Chapters 1-7 of Simon During, *Foucault and Literature: Towards a Genealogy of Writing* (London: Routledge, 1992).

10 See During, *Foucault and Literature*, 67ff.

11 During, *Foucault and Literature*, 122.

12 Foucault, "A Conversation with Michel Foucault", *Partisan Review*, Vol. 38, No. 2, (Spring 1971), 201.

13 George Steiner, "The Mandarin of the Hour—Michel Foucault", *New York Times*, February 28, 1971, http://www.nytimes.com/books/00/12/17/specials/foucault-order.html.

14 Daniel Defert, "Chronology" in Christopher Falzon, Timothy O'Leary, and Jana Sawicki eds., *A Companion to Foucault* (Malden Mass.: Wiley-Blackwell, 2013), 41.

SECTION 3
IMPACT

MODULE 9
THE FIRST RESPONSES

KEY POINTS

- An important criticism of Foucault's work is that it appears to be overly deterministic.*

- Despite its later wide circulation, there have been few direct responses to "What is an Author?"

- The most important factors in the essay's reception are its impact on New Historicism and its presence in undergraduate English courses.

Criticism

A curious element in the immediate reception of Michel Foucault's "What is an Author?" was the extent to which it was misunderstood. At its first presentation in France in 1969, the eminent French intellectuals who debated with Foucault directly afterward were, to say the least, skeptical of the paper. This was in no small part due to a conviction that the essay repeated Roland Barthes's thesis of the "death of the author."[1]

This was immediately apparent when the floor opened to questions. The novelist Jean d'Ormesson* said that Foucault's central thesis was "the death of man,"* and that this time he had simply "attacked the weakest link in the chain": the author.[2] That is, d'Ormesson felt it was already clear that the "author" cannot be treated as a real person, and regarded Foucault as attacking the idea of fixed human nature. But, d'Ormesson went on to say, "I said to myself that, all the same, there are authors."[3] D'Ormesson was joined in this by philosopher Lucien Goldmann,* who took a more sophisticated route to the same position. He aligned Foucault with "the French

> ❝ What is more: I did not say that the author does not exist; I did not say that, and I am astonished that my discourse could have given rise to such a misinterpretation. ❞
>
> Michel Foucault, in conversation after presenting "Qu'est-ce qu'un auteur?"

school of structuralism" as exemplified by Claude Lévi-Strauss, Roland Barthes, Louis Althusser, and Jacques Derrida.[4]

With this in mind, Goldmann asserted that "Michel Foucault is not the author, and certainly not the instaurator* of what he has just said to us."[5] Instead, Goldmann felt that Foucault was simply repeating the overall thesis of his fellow structuralists. Though Goldmann granted Foucault a "particularly original and brilliant" place in that school, he nevertheless made clear his own skepticism of what he saw as their "fundamentally antiscientific philosophical position." [6] Additionally, he added his voice to the idea that Foucault, as a structuralist, was asserting the death of man in general, or, to use the more technical term, of "the subject."* In Goldmann's view, the structuralists believed there was no such thing as fixed human nature, and no such thing as individual freedom of thought, thanks to the influence of social structures. Foucault's paper, he argued, had simply reasserted this with specific regard to "the author" rather than "man" or "the subject."

Responses

Foucault could be extremely blunt in his responses to those he believed were misinterpreting his work.[7] In response to Goldmann, Foucault immediately distanced himself from the structuralists, saying "I have never [...] used the word structure [...] So I would like very much to be spared all these facile remarks about structuralism, or at least ask that the trouble be taken to justify them."[8] Similarly, in response to Goldmann's accusation of being anti-scientific, Foucault said, "Certainly, I am not pretending to have carried out scientific work here, but I would like to know what this reproach is based on."[9]

On the central issue of the author, Foucault was blunter still. As he pointed out, he had simply "not said that the author did not exist." On that count he said, "Let us hold back our tears."[10] Insofar as it related to the supposed "death of man," what Foucault was interested in was the idea that both man and author are historical concepts, formed according to certain rules.[11] It was in this process of formation and in its rules that he was interested.

Foucault saw no reason to alter his stance, or to substantially clarify it after the debate. The fact that he presented "What is an Author?" the following year in English with only minimal edits shows that he stood by both his ideas and their expression.

Conflict and Consensus

"What is an Author?" largely sank without trace in France when it was published, and did not spark any significant ongoing debate in the immediate wake of its presentation. The same is true of the essay's American reception until 1979. With its inclusion that year in Josué Harari's anthology *Textual Strategies: Perspectives in Post-Structuralist Criticism*, "What is an Author?" was slowly absorbed into the canon of literary theory in the English-speaking world. Since then, the essay's reception has been guided by its fixed place on university reading lists and in introductory theory courses. There, it has come to have a status as a seminal contribution to the ongoing theoretical debate around the role, place, and meaning of the author.

That status, however, is complicated by another important defining context: Foucault's own fame and controversial status as one of the best-known intellectuals in the world. By the early 1970s, Foucault was, as the literary critic George Steiner put it in his 1971 review of

The Order of Things, "the mandarin of the hour"—in other words, a fashionable guru.[12] His profile in the United States only rose from then on, especially with the increasingly political bent of his work on punishment and sexuality. This status more than anything else ensured the major–minor status of "What is an Author?" It is an essay bound to be read because of Foucault's importance, and yet bound to be of minor status compared to his books. From the late 1980s, this double status would be exemplified in Foucault's absorption into the movement known as New Historicism.

NOTES

1   Daniel Defert, "Chronology" in Christopher Falzon, Timothy O'Leary, and Jana Sawicki eds., *A Companion to Foucault* (Malden Mass.: Wiley-Blackwell, 2013), 41.

2   Michel Foucault, *Dits et écrits, 1954-1988*, 4 vols., eds. Daniel Defert and François Ewald (Paris: Gallimard, 1994), Vol 1, 812 (my translation).

3   Foucault, *Dits et écrits*, Vol 1, 812.

4   Foucault, *Dits et écrits*, Vol 1, 813.

5   Foucault, *Dits et écrits*, Vol 1, 813.

6   Foucault, *Dits et écrits*, Vol 1, 813.

7   The classic example of Foucault's combativeness in this regard is Michel Foucault, "Polemic: Monstrosities in Criticism", *Diacritics*, Vol. 1, No. 1 (Autumn, 1971), pp. 57-60.

8   Foucault, *Dits et écrits*, Vol 1, 816-17.

9   Foucault, *Dits et écrits*, Vol 1, 816.

10 Foucault, *Dits et écrits*, Vol 1, 817.

11 Foucault, *Dits et écrits*, Vol 1, 817.

12 George Steiner, "The Mandarin of the Hour—Michel Foucault", *New York Times*, February 28, 1971, http://www.nytimes.com/books/00/12/17/specials/foucault-order.html.

MODULE 10
THE EVOLVING DEBATE

KEY POINTS

- In literary studies, the impact of Foucault's work has been most visible among the school of critics known as the New Historicists.*

- New Historicism marked a turn toward a broad consideration of texts in history and in relation to power dynamics in society.

- "What is an Author?" is no t the most influential Foucauldian text for New Historicism, but provides a gateway to some of its central ideas.

Uses and Problems

As noted above, Michel Foucault's "What is an Author?" has a strange double status as a minor work by one of the twentieth century's most influential thinkers. In his later work, Foucault left the essay's questions largely unanswered, preferring to move toward the more general problems posed by his career-defining concern with power and its relation to the individual. He addressed this in far more detail in the major works that followed "What is an Author?" and *The Order of Things*: *Discipline and Punish* and *The History of Sexuality*.

This pattern of moving on is mirrored in debates on authorship more generally. It is a topic that, as literary theorist Seàn Burke* has noted, is doomed to remain open because of the sheer intractability of the figure of the author. As Burke puts it in *The Death and Return of the Author* (1992), "the concept of the author is never more alive than when pronounced dead."[1] In other words, the very concern of figures like Foucault and Roland Barthes to move on from or shift the idea of

> **“** Foucault is the most notable and most pervasive influence on New Historicism. **”**
>
> John Brannigan, *New Historicism and Cultural Materialism*

the author is an index of the author's centrality—and has the tendency to reinforce that centrality.

For some critics, Foucault's skepticism about the author was simply a question of intellectual trendiness, and has often been treated as such. As late as 1992, he was described by one critic as part of "recently fashionable attacks on the concept of the author."[2] Despite the fixed presence of both Barthes and Foucault's essays on student curricula, the day-to-day practice of author-centric literary criticism has often continued much as before, with literary biographies and author studies continuing to be produced for academic and general audiences alike. As Lisa Downing* has noted, this "may be accounted for by the fact that it is simply not easy to 'do' a Foucaldian reading of a piece of literature or other cultural product."[3]

Despite this, however, it is possible to trace Foucault's influence more generally in modern criticism. In particular, the concerns and methodological frameworks that underwrite "What is an Author?" along with Foucault's later work can be seen as the key influence on the school of criticism known as New Historicism.

Schools of Thought

New Historicism rose directly from Foucault's links to the University of California Berkeley—the university that, as François Cusset puts it, became Foucault's "U.S. stronghold."[4] He gave lectures at Berkeley from 1975 onward, and later arranged to spend several months there every year until he died. As the intellectual star of theory in the United States, Foucault's impact at Berkeley is hard to overestimate. In one telling anecdote given by biographer James Miller, Foucault's fame on the Berkeley campus was such that in 1980 students who could not fit into one of his lectures formed an angry mob that had to be calmed by police.[5]

Among those interested in Foucault's work at Berkeley was, by his own testimony, Stephen Greenblatt,* who had been teaching literature there since 1969.[6] Greenblatt's work took direct inspiration from Foucault, and from the 1980s it went on to have a formative effect on contemporary criticism.[7] Greenblatt's *Renaissance Self-Fashioning* (1980), which is regarded as one of New Historicism's founding texts, has an overriding interest in an explicitly Foucauldian examination of texts. As Greenblatt makes clear in the book's epilogue, his work relies on the insight that the human subject is "the ideological product of the relations of power in a particular society."[8] His focus, therefore, was on analyzing the discourses that control this process, whether they be literary or non-literary, authored or un-authored.

Though Greenblatt's work does not explicitly rely on "What is an Author?" for inspiration, the conditions and preconditions of authorship remain a central point of focus. As Michael Payne has noted, Greenblatt's New Historicist work could hardly help but be strongly influenced by a notion of authorship "closely allied" to Foucault's, as shown in "What is an Author?"[9] This is demonstrated by Greenblatt's overriding interest in the social and historical contingencies behind the subject and the acts of reading and writing. Greenblatt, though, is notably more interested than Foucault in carefully examining historical specifics, and in providing literary-critical readings through those specifics.

In Current Scholarship

It is questionable whether the key practitioners of New Historicism today, such as Stephen Greenblatt and Catherine Gallagher,* would regard themselves as drawing directly on "What is an Author?" The deliberately mixed theoretical bases of New Historicism, which draws not only on Foucault's work, but on that of anthropologist Clifford Geertz* and Marxist literary theorist Raymond Williams,* among others, make it hard to draw links to specific texts. But it remains clear, nevertheless, that "What is an Author?" can be seen retrospectively as a kind of manifesto for New Historicism. This is due to its diminished focus on the literary and on the individual author, and its expanded focus on the social conditions of discourse.

Through this, it is possible to see "What is an Author?" as one of the key precedents for what is perhaps the most widely practiced form of literary criticism today. While New Historicism has often proven difficult to define—with even Greenblatt himself denying that it was ever strictly a school at all—it is widely agreed to have had a formative influence over literary criticism since the publication of *Renaissance Self-Fashioning*.[10] While its influence has been particularly notable among specialists in early modern literary studies, it is hard to deny that, as Mark Robson* notes, "new historicism has become the dominant mode of literary criticism in the Anglophone world since its emergence in the 1980s."[11] While the author figure still remains a central figure in modern criticism, the theoretical bases of New Historicism have helped make critics far less ready to treat him or her as they once did.

NOTES

1   Seàn Burke, *The Death and Return of the Author: Criticism and Subjectivity in Barthes, Foucault and Derrida* (Edinburgh: Edinburgh University Press, 1992), 7.

2   David Ellis, "Review: *The Death and Return of the Author: Criticism and Subjectivity in Barthes, Foucault and Derrida* by Seàn Burke", *Cambridge Quarterly*, 22 (3), 331.

3   Lisa Downing, *the Cambridge Introduction to Foucault* (Cambridge: Cambridge University Press, 2008), 53.

4   François Cusset, *French Theory: How Foucault, Derrida, Deleuze, & Co. Transformed the Intellectual Life of the United States*, trans. Jeff Fort, Josephine Berganza and Marlon Jones (Mineapolis: University of Minnesota Press, 2008), 162.

5   James Miller, *The Passion of Michel Foucault* (New York: Simon & Schuster, 1993), 321.

6   See Stephen Greenblatt, "Towards a poetics of culture", *Southern Review*, volume 20, no. 1, March 1987, pp. 3-15: 3.

7   See Cusset, *French Theory*, 162, and John Brannigan, *New Historicism and Cultural Materialism* (Basingstoke: Macmillan, 1998), 42.

8   Stephen Greenblatt, *Renaissance Self-Fashioning: From More to Shakespeare* (Chicago: Chicago University Press, 1980), 256.

9   Stephen Greenblatt, *The Greenblatt Reader*, ed. Michael Payne (Oxford: Blackwell, 2005), 1.

10 For a potted history and overview of the key texts in New Historicism, see H. Aram Veeser ed., *The New Historicism* (London: Routledge, 1989).

11 See Mark Robson, "New Historicism" in Gregory Castle, Robert Eaglestone, and M. Keith Booker eds., *The Encyclopedia of Literary and Cultural Theory* (Chichester: Wiley-Blackwell, 2011), 746.

MODULE 11
IMPACT AND INFLUENCE TODAY

KEY POINTS

- "What is an Author?" is a fixture on introductory theory courses in the English-speaking world.

- The concept of the author function has proven challenging for many literary scholars to put into practice in their own work.

- In many ways, the idea of the author function has been quietly ignored in mainstream literary criticism.

Position

Michel Foucault's "What is an Author?" remains a key touchstone for students of literary theory across the English–speaking world, particularly for students of Foucault. The essay has been a fixture in Foucault anthologies in the United States and remains a key part of his legacy for literary theory. It has appeared in anthologies from 1977's *Language, Counter-Memory, Practice*,[1] which was the first anthology of Foucault's work published in the United States, through to 2003's *The Essential Foucault*.[2] It is also a fixture alongside Roland Barthes's "The Death of the Author" in general anthologies of literary theory.[3]

Despite this, the essay's sustained influence on literary criticism has proven limited. In many ways, the late-1960s arguments about authorial intention have died down. While Foucault's author function is often regarded as the most sophisticated and suggestive of the theses put forward, it has also proven an unwieldy concept to put to use. With a continuous output of literary biography, life-studies,

> ❝ At least some of the astounding implausibility of [Foucault's] view is only apparent. ❞
> Alexander Nehamas, "What an Author Is"

and otherwise author-centered critical works, the mainstream of criticism has continued working quite happily with the figure of the author.

The author function has nevertheless proven useful as a means of situating authorship in specific historical contexts. As Jürgen Pieters has noted regarding Stephen Greenblatt's New Historicism, Foucault's conception of authorship brings with it an "immediate advantage" for certain forms of criticism. It "takes into account the social and historical determinations of the authorial position and the rules and regulations that delimit the discursive field in which the author operates."[4] In other words, it allows, or perhaps even forces, the historically aware critic to take into account the forces authors must negotiate in order to produce their work.

Interaction

In large part, the debates around "What is an Author?" that took place from the late 1980s onward mirrored the debate that immediately followed the lecture's first delivery at the Collège de France in 1969. Like that audience, many critics who have objected to Foucault's position have simply lumped it together with Roland Barthes's "The Death of the Author." When not forthrightly indignant, the responses to this presumed position have been skeptical.

In one way or another, many have responded, that "reports of the death of the author have been greatly exaggerated."[5] The standard arc—as seen in studies by philosopher William Irwin* and literary theorist Seàn Burke—has been to situate Barthes and Foucault together at the beginning of a narrative that begins with the death of the author and ends in with his coming back to life. Hence the titles of Burke's *The Death and Return of the Author: Criticism and Subjectivity* in Barthes, Foucault and Derrida* (1992),[6] and Irwin's skeptical anthology *The Death and Resurrection of the Author.*[7]

Even the most Foucauldian literary critic working today has charted a similar trajectory in his consideration of authorship. Where Stephen Greenblatt's work once held a pragmatic sense that authorship was a complex matter of "negotiation between a creator or a class of creators, equipped with a complex, communally shared repertoire of conventions, and the institutions and practices of society," he has since written far more popular studies that fully centralize the old notion of authorship and biographical literary criticism.[8] The most notable of these is 2004's intensely author-centric *Will in the World: How Shakespeare Became Shakespeare.*[9]

The Continuing Debate

As Seàn Burke noted in the preface to the second edition of his *Death and Return of the Author,* by the late 1990s, authorship remained "a centre of controversy," but that that controversy was "becoming an indexed item in the literary and cultural encyclopedia rather than the shortfall of theoretical, political, or historicist programmes."[10] Put simply, the argument was seen as an historical event, rather than a continuing question for critics to address. Despite this, Burke saw the possibility for further research on authorship and on "the relation between human agency and knowledge."[11]

The latter of these areas is precisely the crux of Foucault's life's work as a theorist. Though Burke's own stance is far removed from Foucault's "author function," he is well aware of the insights to be found within "What is an Author?" Indeed, many of these insights, either drawn from the essay itself or from Foucault's work as a whole, are now fixtures in literary criticism. Foucault's work has been absorbed both into studies on the history of the book and on the legal and material conditions of authorship.[12] It also features in several more philosophically-orientated studies of authorial ethics and subjectivity.[13]

The place of "What is an Author?" itself is elegantly summed up by Burke' response to its central question in his *Ethics of Writing*. To "What does it matter who is speaking?" he answers, "Societies are not […] likely to lose interest in who is speaking. The commercial fortunes of biography in our day and age would alone testify to the fact that the demand to retrace a work to its author is virtually as powerful as that to retrace a crime to its perpetrator, a murdered body to its murderer."[14]

NOTES

1 Michel Foucault, *Language, Counter-Memory, Practice*, ed. and trans. Donald F. Bouchard and Sherry Simon (Ithaca, NY: Cornell University Press, 1977).

2 Michel Foucault, *The Essential Foucault*, edited by Paul Rabinow and Nikolas Rose (New York: New Press, 2003).

3 See, e.g. Vincent B. Leitch ed., *The Norton Anthology of Theory and Criticism*, 2nd ed. (New York ; London: W. W. Norton, 2010).

4 Jürgen Pieters, *Moments of Negotiation: The New Historicism of Stephen Greenblatt* (Amsterdam: Amsterdam University Press, 2001), 35.

5 Donald Keefer, "Reports of the Death of the Author", *Philosophy and Literature*, vol. 19 no. 1, 1995, 78.

6 Seàn Burke, *The Death and Return of the Author: Criticism and Subjectivity in Barthes, Foucault and Derrida*, 3rd ed. (Edinburgh: Edinburgh University Press, 2008).

7 William Irwin ed., *The Death and Resurrection of the Author?* (Westport, Connecticut: Greenwood Press, 2002).

8 Stephen Greenblatt, "Towards a poetics of culture", *Southern Review*, volume 20, no. 1, March 1987, 13.

9 See Stephen Greenblatt, *Will in the World: How Shakespeare Became Shakespeare* (London: The Bodley Head, 2014).

10 Burke, *Death and Return of the Author*, ix.

11   Burke, *Death and Return of the Author*, ix.

12   See, e.g., Foucault's place in David Finkelstein and Alistair McCleery eds., *The Book History Reader*, 2nd edition (London: Routledge, 2006).

13   Seàn Burke, *The Ethics of Writing: Authorship and Legacy in Plato and Nietzsche* (Edinburgh: Edinburgh University Press, 2008).

14   Burke, *Ethics of Writing*, 21.

WHERE NEXT?

KEY POINTS

- "What is an Author?" remains a key touchstone text whenever authorship comes under theoretical scrutiny.

- The impact of "What is an Author?" lies in drawing attention to the changing social, legal, and discursive conditions of writing.

- "What is an Author?" is a seminal text both as a pathway into theories of authorship and into Foucault's work more generally.

Potential

Michel Foucault's "What is an Author?" has often come under strong criticism in the years since its first publication, but it remains an unavoidable text in any discussion of authorship and intention* in art. Foucault's own authorial fame is—perhaps ironically—crucial to the essay's continued place in literary studies, but there is more to it than that. As Seàn Burke noted in the third edition of his *Death and Return of the Author* (2008), the questions that surround the place and status of the author in literary studies are far from settled, even if the pragmatic stance of day-to-day scholarship tends to minimize them. Speaking of his own work, Burke notes that every reconsideration of authorship seems to raise new questions, and that "with every revisiting the space of authorship enlarges."[1]

In no small part, the continuing appeal of Foucault's work lies precisely in its refusal to settle on a specific point of view, in favor of posing a set of questions and a paradigm—"the author function"—for posing further questions still. What Burke terms the "irreducible

> **"** [I]f the term 'author' is to serve as a helpful descriptive or explanatory tool in a context of systematic enquiry and scholarly debate, we need a consensus on a more limited and cogent usage. The absence of such a consensus [...] has fuelled confusion in the theoretical literature on authorship. **"**
>
> Paisley Livingston,* *Art and Intention*

singularity of every authorial act," demands as many theories of authorship as there are authors themselves. "What is an Author?" draws attention to precisely that idea. As such, it is likely to continue to be reread by scholars and philosophers looking for new ways to consider authorship. Particularly as the idea of authorship itself is reshaped by new laws, new technologies, and the new social structures that will emerge from them.

Future Directions

The internet is foremost among the new contexts in which "What is an Author?" is primed to provide new theoretical insights and avenues of inquiry. The advent of a new mode of publishing has seen a vast proliferation of both authors and ideas of authorship. These have formed in response to new freedoms of speech and new forms of censorship—all of which beg the question "What is an author?" anew. Given the constant flux of the web's development across the world, with the shifting and contested status of net neutrality and international copyright laws, that proliferation seems unlikely to stop any time soon.

Among those working on authorship today are many experts and theoreticians across several fields. They are working in the wake of scholars such as art historian Molly Nesbitt*[2] and legal scholar David Lange*[3] who were already readdressing the questions in Foucault's essay from the late 1980s onward. More recently, Mark Poster* has used Foucault and "What is an Author?" to examine authority and the "digital subject."*[4] Elsewhere, analytical philosophers such as William Irwin—who is deeply skeptical of what he terms Foucault's "anti-realist" position[5]—are still forced to deal with "What is an Author?" in their discussions of intention.[6]

It is, of course, hard to predict what new authorial contexts will open themselves up to scrutiny in the age of new media. What seems certain, though, is that with the continuous proliferation of hybrid forms such as the internet novel, and of new channels for publishing such as internet forums and e-publishing, authorship will continue to be the object of theoretical debates. In those, "What is an Author?" shows no sign of disappearing. Indeed, as shown by the title of Irwin's study *Intentionalist Interpretation: A Philosophical Explanation and Defense*, Foucault's work, along with Roland Barthes's, retains enough force that theorists are still tussling with it today. In short, as Seàn Burke puts it, "Authorial theory is 'still to come.'"[7]

Summary

Foucault is widely agreed to be one of the most influential philosophers and theoreticians of the twentieth century. As Jonathan Arac put it in 1992, even where Foucault's work has been "severely criticized as an obstacle to effective understanding," it "has changed the basis for the work of all scholars" in the humanities.[8] Within the massive corpus of Foucault's work as a whole, "What is an Author?" remains a minor piece. Nevertheless, it is a crucial touchstone for students of literature, both as a means of understanding the ongoing debates about the author and authorial intention in literary works, and as a way into Foucault's work.

Central to the essay's place as a key text in authorship theory is its careful charting of a third way between the traditional author-centric or intentionalist* theories and the radical anti-authorial stance laid out by Roland Barthes in "The Death of the Author." Foucault's persistent call to attend both to historical specifics and theoretical possibilities is exemplified perfectly in "What is an Author?" As such, it is a text that retains the status of a classic even for its fiercest critics. In Seàn Burke's words, the essay continues to present us with a wealth of "unexploited questions."[9] Even today, the question of what an author is persists.

NOTES

1   Seàn Burke, *The Ethics of Writing: Authorship and Legacy in Plato and Nietzsche*, (Edinburgh: Edinburgh University Press, 2008), xx.

2   See, e.g., Molly Nesbit, "What Was an Author?", *Yale French Studies*, No. 73, Everyday Life (1987), pp. 229-257.

3   For representative work by David Lange, citing Foucault, see David Lange Play in the Fields of the Word: Copyright and the Construction of Authorship in the Post-Literate Millennium", *Law and Contemporary Problems*, Vol. 55, No. 2, Copyright and Legislation: The Kastenmeier Years (Spring, 1992), pp. 139-151; and, for a more general discussion, David Lange and H. Jefferson Powell, *No Law : Intellectual Property in the Image of an Absolute First Amendment* (Stanford, CA: Stanford Law Books, 2009).

4   See Mark Poster, "The Digital Subject and Cultural Theory", in *The Book History Reader*, 2nd ed., eds. David Finkelstein and Alistair McCleery (London: Routledge, 2006); and, for a deeper, broader analysis, Mark Poster, *What's Wrong with the Internet* (Minneapolis: University of Minnesota Press, 2001).

5   See Paisley Livingston, (*Art and Intention: A Philosophical Study*, Oxford: Clarendon Press, 2005), p. 67.

6   For a general summary of analytical philosophical positions on authorship see William Irwin "Internationalism and Author Constructs" in William Irwin ed., *The Death and Resurrection of the Author* (Westport CT: Greenwood Press, 2002), 191-204.

7   Seàn Burke, *The Death and return of the author: criticism and subjectivity in Barthes, Foucault and Derrida*, 3rd ed. (Edinburgh: Edinburgh University Press, 2008), xxii.

8   Jonathan Arac ed., *After Foucault: Humanistic Knowledge, Postmodern Challenges* (New Brunswick: Rutgers University Press, 1988).

9   Burke, *Death and Return*, 228, n. 22.

GLOSSARY

GLOSSARY OF TERMS

Algerian War (1954-1962): sometimes called the Algerian War of Independence or Algerian Revolution, the Algerian War was a conflict between France and revolutionaries in the North African French colony of Algeria. It was characterized by extreme brutality by the French army and by the use of torture by both government forces and the FLN (Algerian National Liberation Front). The war had a huge impact on domestic politics in France and precipitated the end of the Fourth Republic. It culminated in the granting of Algerian independence in mid-1962.

Author Function: a term coined by Michel Foucault to describe how certain kinds of text or discourse are assigned an "author" rather than a "scriptor" or anonymous text producer.

Authorial Intention: the assumed intent, purpose, desired outcome, or desired communicative effect present in an author's mind when writing a text. In the simplest terms, it is what the writer wanted to say or the effect the writer wanted to create.

Book history: the branch of history and literary criticism which deals with the material history of writing, publication, and printing as it relates to our understanding of texts and their circulation in society.

Collège de France: a research university in Paris, France. It was founded in 1530 and gives free public lectures for anyone who wishes to attend. As one of the most famous centers of learning and research in France, election to a professorship there is among the highest accolades given by the French university system. Teaching at the Collège is publically recognized as a sign of being one of France's foremost intellectuals.

Communication studies: a branch of social sciences which analyzes the different processes of human communication and their circulation in society. It uses theoretic bases which range from mathematics and statistics through to linguistics, semiology, and sociology.

Communism: a political philosophy drawn substantially from the work of Karl Marx. It holds that society should be structured around the common ownership of resources and the means of production, and organized around total equality.

Death of man: sometimes also called "death of the subject,"* "death of man" is a term for the philosophical position that there is no such thing as fixed human nature. Philosophers and theorists who take this position are often termed "anti-humanist." A belief in the "death of man" maintains that human nature or individual personhood is determined by the social and economic conditions of society (see determinism).* Michel Foucault is perhaps the most famous philosopher associated with the "death of man" in the twentieth century. The term is often used pejoratively by critics of structuralism, post-structuralism, and deconstruction.

Death of the author: a theory which stems from French theorist Roland Barthes's* 1968 essay of the same name. It refers to the stance that readers, rather than authors, generate meaning in texts, and that, by writing, the author in some sense "dies."

Decolonization: the process by which nations holding colonies overseas withdraw from those colonies and grant them independence. It is particularly associated with the breakup of the British Empire and the French Empire in the years following World War II.

Deconstruction: a term drawn from the work of French philosopher Jacques Derrida.* It is a school of thought that focuses on the instability of language and the impossibility of fixing meaning. It is particularly associated with post-structuralism.*

Determinism: any philosophical or scientific stance that holds that a given set of conditions can only have one possible outcome. In reference to Marxist,* structuralist,* and anti-humanist (see "death of man")* theory, determinism applies particularly to the notion that historical conditions determine human subjectivity* in a process that individuals have no power to counteract.

Deterministic: see Determinism

Discourse: any form of written or spoken communication. It also includes specific subsets of specialized language groups such as scientific discourse or legal discourse. In the work of Michel Foucault, discourse fulfills several functions. However, it is particularly used to examine how the limitations of communications and their interactions with social power dynamics define and restrict possibilities for subject* formation, knowledge, and human agency.

École Normale Supérieure (ENS): based in Paris, the ENS is one of the most prestigious higher-education institutions in France, if not the most prestigious. Founded in 1794 to train teachers, it is highly selective and is the *alma mater* of an astonishing percentage of France's most famous intellectuals and politicians.

Feminism: the set of movements and ideologies seeking to achieve equality for women.

French Communist Party: see PCF.

French Liberation (1944-1945): the freeing of France from Nazi German rule during World War II.

French Socialists: English name for the *Parti socialiste*, a center-left political party in France founded in 1905. During the 1960s it was the major left-wing force in French politics.

French Structuralism: see structuralism.

French Theory: a catch-all term often employed by historians of late twentieth-century thought. It refers to the body of work produced by influential thinkers in structuralism* and poststructuralism* during the 1960s and 1970s. Though there is no defined corpus or single outlook associated with French theory, it is closely associated with the work of Michel Foucault and Jacques Derrida,* among others.

Governmentality: a concept developed by Michel Foucault in his later work. Governmentality refers to the ways in which governments attempt to produce citizens suitable for them to govern.

***Hamlet*:** written 1599-1602, *The Tragedy of Hamlet, Prince of Denmark* is a tragedy by William Shakespeare.* It is the most famous play in the English language.

Historicism: any approach to analysis that seeks to interpret the object or subject via the particular historical conditions of the time and society in which it first appeared.

Historicist: see Historicism

History of science: the subset of history that analyzes the emergence and formation of scientific theories and discourse across human history.

Human Sciences: a term, more generally in use in Continental Europe, for the full range of subjects in the humanities and social sciences, including but not limited to literary studies, anthropology, sociology, and philosophy.

Ideological State Apparatuses: a term coined by French Marxist theorist Louis Althusser* for the state-run institutions that communicate and instill the ideology of the state, thereby making citizens conform to the ruling ideology. ISAs include churches, schools, universities, and so on.

The Iliad: an Ancient Greek epic attributed to Homer* which recounts the events of the Fall of Troy. Traditionally, its composition is dated to c. 850 B.C.E..

Instaurator: a rare term used by Michel Foucault to designate figures credited with founding a specific discourse.* E.g. Sigmund Freud,* father of psychoanalysis.

Intention: see authorial intention.

Intentional Fallacy: a term coined by William Wimsatt* and Monroe Beardsley* which suggests that it is incorrect to treat authorial intention* as the basis of interpretation or critical judgement.

Lycée: French high-school.

Marxism: a broad political, intellectual, and philosophical school based around the theories of German philosopher, economist, and revolutionary socialist Karl Marx. Strongly associated with Communism, Marxism provides a range of ways for analyzing the relations between culture, society, and economics.

Marxist: see Marxism

May 1968: a period of extreme civil unrest in France characterized by vast student protests, strikes, and public protests. May 1968 is frequently referred to as a watershed in modern French history.

New Criticism: a mid-twentieth century school of literary criticism which takes its name from the eponymous 1941 study by critic John Crowe-Ransom. New Critics, including William Wimsatt* and Monroe Beardsley,* advocated extremely close attention to texts and their forms, often over context and authorial intention.

New Critics: see New Criticism

New Historicism: a late twentieth century school of criticism in literature, art, and cultural history that seeks to understand its objects of analysis through their social and cultural contexts. It is closely associated with the work of Stephen Greenblatt* at the University of California, Berkeley. New Historicism flourished during the 1980s and remains to some extent the dominant mode of modern literary criticism.

New Historicist: see New Historicism

Nouvelle critique: a term associated with structuralist* literary criticism in France during the 1950s and 1960s, particularly the work of Roland Barthes.*

The Odyssey: an ancient Greek epic poem recounting the long journey of Odysseus, king of Ithaca, returning home after the events of the Trojan War. Traditionally attributed to Homer, it is dated to c. 750–700 B.C.E..

PCF / Parti Communiste Français: the French communist party, founded in 1920. Still an active force in French politics, the PCF was particularly powerful from 1945-1960, when many of France's public intellectuals were vocal members.

Postmodernism: the general name given to the outlook of various schools of thought in literary theory, philosophy, and sociology that focus particularly on the socially-constructed nature of reality. Foucault is widely regarded as the most influential figure in postmodern theory.

Post-structuralism: a philosophical or theoretic school generally held to have been founded by Jacques Derrida.* Post-structuralism grew out of structuralism,* but was opposed to that school's determinism.* Instead, it proposed a radically open-ended approach to meaning and interpretation.

Queer theory: a broad field of postmodernist* and poststructuralist* theory associated with both LBGTQ studies and women's studies. Often directly inspired by Michel Foucault's structuralist* theory, it is particularly concerned with inquiry into power, social construction, and the nature of identity categories.

Russian Formalists: a group of Russian literary critics particularly influential during the 1920s and 1930s that included Roman Jakobson, Vladimir Propp, and Viktor Shklovsky. Russian Formalism was one of the most significant critical schools of the early twentieth century. It focused on establishing what differentiated formal literary language from everyday language.

Société française de philosophie: a philosophical society founded in France in 1901, dedicated to bringing philosophers together to discuss their research and ideas.

Structuralism: a methodology or theoretical stance drawn originally from structural linguistics as elaborated by Ferdinand de Saussure.* Structuralism seeks to uncover the structures that lie underneath elements of human culture and define how those elements become intelligible to other humans. It is particularly associated with the influential French theorists of the 1950s and 1960s, including Claude Lévi-Strauss* and Roland Barthes.*

Subject: philosophical term for the individual person; hence "subjectivity," meaning the status of being a person, or having "personhood."

PEOPLE MENTIONED IN THE TEXT

Louis Althusser (1918–1990) was a French-Algerian Marxist*
philosopher. He was educated at the École Normale Supérieure* in
Paris, where he later taught. A member of the French Communist
Party,* he was one of the foremost contributors to Marxist theory in
post-war France. Althusser was also an important influence on many
intellectuals, including Michel Foucault. Major works include *For
Marx* (1965) and *Reading Capital* (1965).

Aristotle (384–322 B.C.E.) was an Ancient Greek philosopher and
scientist known for his works on ethics, poetry, theater, physics, and
logic. Major surviving works include *Poetics*, *Physics*, and *Nicomachean
Ethics*.

Roland Barthes (1915–1980) was an influential French literary
theorist, critic, linguist, and semiotician particularly active during the
1950s and 1960s. He was famous for his controversial stances on
traditional critical approaches, including his infamous "death of the
author"* thesis. He was a close friend of Michel Foucault and was a
fellow at the Collège de France* from 1976 until his death in 1980.
Major works include *Writing, Degree Zero* (1953), *Mythologies* (1957)
and *S/Z* (1970), as well as the essay "The Death of the Author" (1968).

Monroe C. Beardsley (1915–1985) was an American literary critic
and philosopher of art who, along with William K. Wimsatt,*
developed the intentional fallacy.* Major works include *Aesthetics*
(1958) and, with Wimsatt, the essays "The Intentional Fallacy" (1946)
and "The Affective Fallacy" (1949).

Samuel Beckett (1906-1989) was a Nobel Prize-winning Irish playwright, novelist, and director who is regarded as one of the most important writers of the mid-late twentieth century. Based in Paris for most of his adult life, he wrote many of his major works in French. Major works include the trilogy of novels *Molloy, Malone Dies,* and *The Unnamable* (1951, 1951, 1953), and the plays *Waiting for Godot* (1953) and *Endgame* (1957) which helped reshape post-war theater.

Seàn Burke (b. 1965) is a literary theorist and novelist best known for his studies on authorship and authorial intention, including *The Death and Return of the Author: Criticism and Subjectivity in Barthes, Foucault and Derrida* (1990).

Antoine Compagnon (b. 1950) is a French literary critic and theorist. Currently Professor of French Literature at the Collège de France,* he is best known for *Le Démon de la théorie* (1998) and *Les Antimodernes, de Joseph de Maistre à Roland Barthes* (2005).

François Cusset (b. 1969) is a French writer and intellectual historian who teaches at the University of Naterre, France; he is best known for his 2003 study *French Theory: How Foucault, Derrida, Deleuze, & Co Transformed the Intellectual Life of the United States.*

Charles de Gaulle (1890-1970) was a French general and politician. He rose to international prominence as the leader and hero of Free France during the Nazi German occupation in World War II. He then became a key figure in post-war conservative French politics. In 1958, he founded the French Fifth Republic with a new constitution and became the first president of France. He held this position from 1959-1969 when he resigned in the wake of the May 1968* crisis.

Gilles Deleuze (1925–1995) was an influential French philosopher and theorist associated with post-structuralism.* A friend and collaborator of Michel Foucault, Deleuze was one of the most influential figures of French intellectual life in the 1960s. Major works include *Difference and Repetition* (1968) and *Anti-Oedipus* (1977), which was written in collaboration with Félix Guattari.

Jacques Derrida (1930–2004) was a French–Algerian Jewish philosopher known as the father of post-structuralism* and deconstruction.* Major works include *Of Grammatology* (1967) and *Writing and Difference* (1967).

Jean d'Ormesson (1925–2017) was a French novelist known for his autobiographical novels. Educated at the École Normale Supérieure, he was a major figure in French literary life from the 1950s onwards. His major works include *The Glory of the Empire* (1971).

Ferdinand de Saussure (1857–1913) was a Swiss linguist and semiotician known above all for founding structural linguistics. His major work is the *Course in General Linguistics* which was published posthumously in 1916.

Lisa Downing (b. 1974) is Professor of French Discourses of Sexuality at the University of Birmingham.

Sigmund Freud (1856–1939) was an Austrian neurologist famous as the founder of psychoanalysis, which was one of the major medical and intellectual movements of the twentieth century. Though many of his theories have been discredited, his work remains a formative influence in many areas of intellectual life, including literary theory. Major works include *The Interpretation of Dreams* (1900) and *Civilization and its Discontents* (1930).

Galen (c.e.129-c.200) was a Greek doctor and philosopher famous for his accomplishments and discoveries in medicine.

Catherine Gallagher (b. 1945) is a New Historicist* literary critic and Professor of English at the University of California, Berkeley. She helped shape New Historicism along with Stephen Greenblatt.* Major works include *Practicing New Historicism* (2000, with Stephen Greenblatt).

Clifford Geertz (1926-2006) was an American anthropologist best known for his work on symbols and his elaboration of "thick description." He was an influential figure in anthropology and also helped shape New Historicism's* approach to literature. His most influential book was *The Interpretation of Cultures* (1973).

Lucien Goldmann (1913-1970) was a French philosopher, Marxist* theorist, and sociologist originally from Romania. Though he was a key figure in the structuralist* school, he was also one of its most prominent critics. His major works include *Towards a Sociology of the Novel* (1964).

Stephen Greenblatt (b. 1943) is an American literary critic and intellectual historian who specializes in renaissance literature. As one of the founders of New Historicism,* he remains best known within academia for *Renaissance Self-Fashioning: From More to Shakespeare*. He is also now known for his popular non-fiction and rose to international prominence outside academia with *Will in the World: How Shakespeare became Shakespeare* (2005) and *The Swerve: How the World Became Modern* (2011).

Josué V. Harari is a professor of French and Italian at Emory University. He specializes in the history of criticism and theory.

Homer is the conventional name given in Ancient Greece to the supposed author of the *Iliad** and the *Odyssey.** Though both poems were almost certainly composed in the late eighth to early seventh centuries B.C.E., it is debatable whether they were composed by a single writer.

William Irwin (b. 1970) is an American philosopher whose early work, including *Intentionalist Interpretation: A Philosophical Explanation and Defense* (1999) examined authorial intention* and intentionalism.* He is now better known for his books on philosophy and popular culture including *Seinfeld and Philosophy: A Book about Everything and Nothing* (2000).

Julia Kristeva (b. 1941) is a Bulgarian-French feminist philosopher, literary critic, and psychoanalyst. She is best known for her structuralist work on literature and linguistics, above all the elaboration of intertextuality in books such as *Desire in Language: A Semiotic Approach to Literature and Art* (1969).

Jacques Lacan (1901–1981) was a French psychoanalyst and philosopher whose work was highly influential in the 1960s and 1970s. He is best known for *Écrits* (1966).

David L. Lange is an American legal scholar who specializes in intellectual property and copyright.

Claude Lévi-Strauss (1908–2009) was an influential French anthropologist who is credited with founding structural anthropology and exerting a formative influence on structuralism in post-war France. Major works include *Tristes Tropiques* (1955), *Structural Anthropology* (1958), and *The Savage Mind* (1962).

Paisley Livingston is a Canadian philosopher and aesthetician known for his work on intentionalism, film, and art, including *Art and Intention: A Philosophical Study* (2005).

Molly Nesbit is an American art historian and critic. She is a professor of Art at Vassar College and is best known for her work on contemporary art, film, and photography. *Pragmatism in the History of Art* (2013) is the first volume of her collected essays and lectures.

Raymond Picard (1917-1975) was a French literary critic and scholar of the works of Jean Racine.* He is known for his antipathy to New Criticism,* as expressed in his 1965 book, *Nouvelle critique ou nouvelle imposture* (*New Criticism or New Fraud?*) which was a response to Roland Barthes's* *On Racine* (1963).

Mark Poster (1941-2012) was an American intellectual historian and media theorist. He was Professor Emeritus of History and Film and Media Studies at the University of California Irvine and was a prominent figure in the use of French theory* in the United States. His major works include *Critical Theory and Poststructuralism: In Search of a Context* (1989) and *The Information Subject* (2001).

Jean Racine (1639-1699) was a French playwright who is known as one of the greatest literary figures in French history. Above all, he is known for writing tragedies inspired by the classical tradition. His major works include *Andromaque* (1667) and *Phèdre* (1677).

William Shakespeare (1564-1616) was an English poet and playwright who is now known as the national poet of England. The author of approximately 38 plays (counting collaborative works) as well as sonnets and other poems, he is perhaps best known for his

Sonnets (1609) and the great tragedies *Hamlet* (1599–1602) and *Macbeth* (1606).

George Steiner (b. 1929) is a French American literary critic and essayist. A major figure in literary criticism since the 1960s, he remains best known for his books *The Death of Tragedy* (1961) and *After Babel* (1975).

William K. Wimsatt Jr. (1907–1975) was an American literary critic and theorist best known for his contributions to New Criticism. His most well-known essays, written in collaboration with Monroe C. Beardsley, are "The Intentional Fallacy" (1946) and "The Affective Fallacy" (1949). His major essays are collected in *The Verbal Icon: Studies in the Meaning of Poetry* (1954).

WORKS CITED

WORKS CITED

Bawer, Bruce. "The Case of Stephen Greenblatt." In *The New Criterion*, Vol. 36, No. 1. (September 2017).

Brannigan, John. *New Historicism and Cultural Materialism*. Basingstoke: Macmillan, 1998.

Burke, Seàn. *The Death and return of the author: criticism and subjectivity in Barthes, Foucault and Derrida*. 3rd edition. Edinburgh: Edinburgh University Press, 2008.

The Ethics of Writing: Authorship and Legacy in Plato and Nietzsche. Edinburgh: Edinburgh University Press, 2008.

Cusset, François. *French Theory: How Foucault, Derrida, Deleuze, & Co. Transformed the Intellectual Life of the United States*, translated by Jeff Fort, Josephine Berganza and Marlon Jones. Minneapolis: University of Minnesota Press, 2008.

Defert, Daniel. "Chronology" in Christopher Falzon, Timothy O'Leary, and Jana Sawicki eds., *A Companion to Foucault*. Malden Mass.: Wiley-Blackwell, 2013.

Downing, Lisa. *The Cambridge Introduction to Michel Foucault*. Cambridge: Cambridge University Press, 2008.

During, Simon. *Foucault and Literature: Towards a Genealogy of Writing*. London: Routledge, 1992.

Finkelstein, David and McCleery, Alistair eds. *The Book History Reader*. 2nd edition. London: Routledge, 2006.

Foucault, Michel. *L'Archéologie du savoir*. Paris: Gallimard,1969.

The Archaeology of Knowledge and the Discourse on Language, translated by A. M. Sheridan Smith and Rupert Swyer. New York: Pantheon Books, 1972.

The Birth of the Clinic: An Archaeology of Medical Perception, translated by A.M. Sheridan. London: Tavistock, 1973.

"A Conversation with Michel Foucault", *Partisan Review*, Vol. 38, No. 2,. (Spring 1971): 192-201.

Discipline and Punish: The Birth of the Prison, translated by Alan Sheridan. London: Allen Lane, 1977.

Dits et écrits, 1954-1988, 4 volumes., edited by Daniel Defert and François Ewald. Paris: Gallimard, 1994.

The Essential Foucault, edited by Paul Rabinow and Nikolas Rose New York: New Press, 2003.

Histoire de la sexualité, 3 volumes. Paris: Gallimard, 1976-84.

History of Madness, edited by Jean Khalfa, translated by Jonathan Murphy. London: Routledge, 2006.

The History of Sexuality, 3 volumes., translated by Robert Hurley. New York: Pantheon, 1978-86).

Language, Counter-Memory, Practice, edited and translated by Donald F. Bouchard and Sherry Simon. Ithaca, NY: Cornell University Press, 1977.

Les mots et les choses. Une archéologie des sciences humaines. Paris: Gallimard, 1966.

Naissance de la Clinique: une archéologie du regard medical (Paris: Presses Universitaires de France, 1963.

The Order of Things, trans. Anonymous. London: Tavistock, 1970.

"Polemic: Monstrosities in Criticism", *Diacritics*, Vol. 1, No. 1. Autumn, 1971): 57-60.

"Qu'est-ce qu'un auteur?," *Bulletin de la Société française de philosophie*, 63, no. 3, July-September 1969, pp.73-104Greenblatt, Stephen. *The Greenblatt Reader*, edited by Michael Payne. Oxford: Blackwell, 2005.

Renaissance Self-Fashioning: From More to Shakespeare. Chicago: Chicago University Press, 1980.

Surveiller et punir: naissance de la prison. Paris: Gallimard, 1975.

"Towards a poetics of culture", *Southern Review*, Volume 20, no. 1, (March 1987): 3-15.

Will in the World: How Shakespeare Became Shakespeare. London: The Bodley Head, 2014.

Grindon, Gavin and Ryan, Michael. "Marxism" in *The Encyclopedia of Literary and Cultural Theory*, edited by Gregory Castle, Robert Eaglestone, and M. Keith Booker. Chichester: Wiley-Blackwell, 2011.

Gutting, Gary ed., *The Cambridge Companion to Foucault*, 2nd edition. Cambridge: Cambridge University Press, 2005.

Harari, Josué V. "Critical Factions/Critical Fictions" *in Textual Strategies: Perspectives in Post-Structuralist Criticism*, edited by Josué V. Harari. Ithaca: Cornell University Press, 1979.

Harari, Josué V. ed., *Textual Strategies: Perspectives in Post-Structuralist Criticism.* Ithaca: Cornell University Press, 1979.

Irwin, William ed., *The Death and Resurrection of the Author?* Westport, Connecticut: Greenwood Press, 2002.

Keefer, Donald. "Reports of the Death of the Author," *Philosophy and Literature*, vol. 19 no. 1, 1995: 78-84.

Lange, David. "At Play in the Fields of the Word: Copyright and the Construction of Authorship in the Post-Literate Millennium," *Law and Contemporary Problems*, Vol. 55, No. 2, Copyright and Legislation: The Kastenmeier Years (Spring, 1992), pp. 139-151.

Lange, David and Powell, H. Jefferson. *No Law: Intellectual Property in the Image of an Absolute First Amendment.* Stanford, CA: Stanford Law Books, 2009.

Leitch, Vincent B. ed., *The Norton Anthology of Theory and Criticism*, 2nd ed. New York; London: W. W. Norton, 2010.

Logie, John. "1967: The Birth of the 'The Death of the Author,'" *College English*, Vo. 75, No. 5. (May 2013): 493-512.

Lynch, Richard A. "Two Bibliographical Resources for Foucault's Work in English," *Foucault Studies*, No. 1, (December 2004): 71-76

Miller, James. *The Passion of Michel Foucault.* New York: Simon & Schuster, 1993.

Mills, Sara. *Discourse.* London: Routledge, 2004.

Munif, Yasser. "Discourse" in *The Encyclopedia of Literary and Cultural Theory*, edited by Gregory Castle, Robert Eaglestone, and M. Keith Booker. Chichester: Wiley-Blackwell, 2011.

Nehamas, Alexander (1986). "What an Author Is." *Journal of Philosophy* 83. 11): 685-691.

Nesbit, Molly. "What Was an Author?", *Yale French Studies*, No. 73, Everyday Life (1987): 229-257.

Picard, Raymond. *Nouvelle critique ou Nouvelle Imposture.* Paris, Pauvert, 1965.

Pieters, Jürgen. *Moments of Negotiation: The New Historicism of Stephen Greenblatt.* Amsterdam: Amsterdam University Press, 2001.

Poster, Mark. "The Digital Subject and Cultural Theory", in *The Book History Reader*, 2nd ed., edited by David Finkelstein and Alistair McCleery. London: Routledge, 2006.

What's Wrong with the Internet. Minneapolis: University of Minnesota Press, 2001.

Prado, C. G., "Editor's introduction" in *Foucault's Legacy*, edited by C. G. Prado. London: Continuum, 2009.

Robson, Mark. "New Historicism" in *The Encyclopedia of Literary and Cultural Theory*, edited by Gregory Castle, Robert Eaglestone, and M. Keith Booker. Chichester: Wiley-Blackwell, 2011.

Solomon, Jack. "Structuralism" in *The Encyclopedia of Literary and Cultural Theory*, edited by Gregory Castle, Robert Eaglestone, and M. Keith Booker. Chichester: Wiley-Blackwell, 2011.

THE MACAT LIBRARY
BY DISCIPLINE

AFRICANA STUDIES

Chinua Achebe's *An Image of Africa: Racism in Conrad's Heart of Darkness*
W. E. B. Du Bois's *The Souls of Black Folk*
Zora Neale Huston's *Characteristics of Negro Expression*
Martin Luther King Jr's *Why We Can't Wait*
Toni Morrison's *Playing in the Dark: Whiteness in the American Literary Imagination*

ANTHROPOLOGY

Arjun Appadurai's *Modernity at Large: Cultural Dimensions of Globalisation*
Philippe Ariès's *Centuries of Childhood*
Franz Boas's *Race, Language and Culture*
Kim Chan & Renée Mauborgne's *Blue Ocean Strategy*
Jared Diamond's *Guns, Germs & Steel: the Fate of Human Societies*
Jared Diamond's *Collapse: How Societies Choose to Fail or Survive*
E. E. Evans-Pritchard's *Witchcraft, Oracles and Magic Among the Azande*
James Ferguson's *The Anti-Politics Machine*
Clifford Geertz's *The Interpretation of Cultures*
David Graeber's *Debt: the First 5000 Years*
Karen Ho's *Liquidated: An Ethnography of Wall Street*
Geert Hofstede's *Culture's Consequences: Comparing Values, Behaviors, Institutes and Organizations across Nations*
Claude Lévi-Strauss's *Structural Anthropology*
Jay Macleod's *Ain't No Makin' It: Aspirations and Attainment in a Low-Income Neighborhood*
Saba Mahmood's *The Politics of Piety: The Islamic Revival and the Feminist Subject*
Marcel Mauss's *The Gift*

BUSINESS

Jean Lave & Etienne Wenger's *Situated Learning*
Theodore Levitt's *Marketing Myopia*
Burton G. Malkiel's *A Random Walk Down Wall Street*
Douglas McGregor's *The Human Side of Enterprise*
Michael Porter's *Competitive Strategy: Creating and Sustaining Superior Performance*
John Kotter's *Leading Change*
C. K. Prahalad & Gary Hamel's *The Core Competence of the Corporation*

CRIMINOLOGY

Michelle Alexander's *The New Jim Crow: Mass Incarceration in the Age of Colorblindness*
Michael R. Gottfredson & Travis Hirschi's *A General Theory of Crime*
Richard Hermstein & Charles A. Murray's *The Bell Curve: Intelligence and Class Structure in American Life*
Elizabeth Loftus's *Eyewitness Testimony*
Jay Macleod's *Ain't No Makin' It: Aspirations and Attainment in a Low-Income Neighborhood*
Philip Zimbardo's *The Lucifer Effect*

ECONOMICS

Janet Abu-Lughod's *Before European Hegemony*
Ha-Joon Chang's *Kicking Away the Ladder*
David Brion Davis's *The Problem of Slavery in the Age of Revolution*
Milton Friedman's *The Role of Monetary Policy*
Milton Friedman's *Capitalism and Freedom*
David Graeber's *Debt: the First 5000 Years*
Friedrich Hayek's *The Road to Serfdom*
Karen Ho's *Liquidated: An Ethnography of Wall Street*

The Macat Library By Discipline

John Maynard Keynes's *The General Theory of Employment, Interest and Money*
Charles P. Kindleberger's *Manias, Panics and Crashes*
Robert Lucas's *Why Doesn't Capital Flow from Rich to Poor Countries?*
Burton G. Malkiel's *A Random Walk Down Wall Street*
Thomas Robert Malthus's *An Essay on the Principle of Population*
Karl Marx's *Capital*
Thomas Piketty's *Capital in the Twenty-First Century*
Amartya Sen's *Development as Freedom*
Adam Smith's *The Wealth of Nations*
Nassim Nicholas Taleb's *The Black Swan: The Impact of the Highly Improbable*
Amos Tversky's & Daniel Kahneman's *Judgment under Uncertainty: Heuristics and Biases*
Mahbub Ul Haq's *Reflections on Human Development*
Max Weber's *The Protestant Ethic and the Spirit of Capitalism*

FEMINISM AND GENDER STUDIES

Judith Butler's *Gender Trouble*
Simone De Beauvoir's *The Second Sex*
Michel Foucault's *History of Sexuality*
Betty Friedan's *The Feminine Mystique*
Saba Mahmood's *The Politics of Piety: The Islamic Revival and the Feminist Subject*
Joan Wallach Scott's *Gender and the Politics of History*
Mary Wollstonecraft's *A Vindication of the Rights of Woman*
Virginia Woolf's *A Room of One's Own*

GEOGRAPHY

The Brundtland Report's *Our Common Future*
Rachel Carson's *Silent Spring*
Charles Darwin's *On the Origin of Species*
James Ferguson's *The Anti-Politics Machine*
Jane Jacobs's *The Death and Life of Great American Cities*
James Lovelock's *Gaia: A New Look at Life on Earth*
Amartya Sen's *Development as Freedom*
Mathis Wackernagel & William Rees's *Our Ecological Footprint*

HISTORY

Janet Abu-Lughod's *Before European Hegemony*
Benedict Anderson's *Imagined Communities*
Bernard Bailyn's *The Ideological Origins of the American Revolution*
Hanna Batatu's *The Old Social Classes And The Revolutionary Movements Of Iraq*
Christopher Browning's *Ordinary Men: Reserve Police Batallion 101 and the Final Solution in Poland*
Edmund Burke's *Reflections on the Revolution in France*
William Cronon's *Nature's Metropolis: Chicago And The Great West*
Alfred W. Crosby's *The Columbian Exchange*
Hamid Dabashi's *Iran: A People Interrupted*
David Brion Davis's *The Problem of Slavery in the Age of Revolution*
Nathalie Zemon Davis's *The Return of Martin Guerre*
Jared Diamond's *Guns, Germs & Steel: the Fate of Human Societies*
Frank Dikotter's *Mao's Great Famine*
John W Dower's *War Without Mercy: Race And Power In The Pacific War*
W. E. B. Du Bois's *The Souls of Black Folk*
Richard J. Evans's *In Defence of History*
Lucien Febvre's *The Problem of Unbelief in the 16th Century*
Sheila Fitzpatrick's *Everyday Stalinism*

Eric Foner's *Reconstruction: America's Unfinished Revolution, 1863-1877*
Michel Foucault's *Discipline and Punish*
Michel Foucault's *History of Sexuality*
Francis Fukuyama's *The End of History and the Last Man*
John Lewis Gaddis's *We Now Know: Rethinking Cold War History*
Ernest Gellner's *Nations and Nationalism*
Eugene Genovese's *Roll, Jordan, Roll: The World the Slaves Made*
Carlo Ginzburg's *The Night Battles*
Daniel Goldhagen's *Hitler's Willing Executioners*
Jack Goldstone's *Revolution and Rebellion in the Early Modern World*
Antonio Gramsci's *The Prison Notebooks*
Alexander Hamilton, John Jay & James Madison's *The Federalist Papers*
Christopher Hill's *The World Turned Upside Down*
Carole Hillenbrand's *The Crusades: Islamic Perspectives*
Thomas Hobbes's *Leviathan*
Eric Hobsbawm's *The Age Of Revolution*
John A. Hobson's *Imperialism: A Study*
Albert Hourani's *History of the Arab Peoples*
Samuel P. Huntington's *The Clash of Civilizations and the Remaking of World Order*
C. L. R. James's *The Black Jacobins*
Tony Judt's *Postwar: A History of Europe Since 1945*
Ernst Kantorowicz's *The King's Two Bodies: A Study in Medieval Political Theology*
Paul Kennedy's *The Rise and Fall of the Great Powers*
Ian Kershaw's *The "Hitler Myth": Image and Reality in the Third Reich*
John Maynard Keynes's *The General Theory of Employment, Interest and Money*
Charles P. Kindleberger's *Manias, Panics and Crashes*
Martin Luther King Jr's *Why We Can't Wait*
Henry Kissinger's *World Order: Reflections on the Character of Nations and the Course of History*
Thomas Kuhn's *The Structure of Scientific Revolutions*
Georges Lefebvre's *The Coming of the French Revolution*
John Locke's *Two Treatises of Government*
Niccolò Machiavelli's *The Prince*
Thomas Robert Malthus's *An Essay on the Principle of Population*
Mahmood Mamdani's *Citizen and Subject: Contemporary Africa And The Legacy Of Late Colonialism*
Karl Marx's *Capital*
Stanley Milgram's *Obedience to Authority*
John Stuart Mill's *On Liberty*
Thomas Paine's *Common Sense*
Thomas Paine's *Rights of Man*
Geoffrey Parker's *Global Crisis: War, Climate Change and Catastrophe in the Seventeenth Century*
Jonathan Riley-Smith's *The First Crusade and the Idea of Crusading*
Jean-Jacques Rousseau's *The Social Contract*
Joan Wallach Scott's *Gender and the Politics of History*
Theda Skocpol's *States and Social Revolutions*
Adam Smith's *The Wealth of Nations*
Timothy Snyder's *Bloodlands: Europe Between Hitler and Stalin*
Sun Tzu's *The Art of War*
Keith Thomas's *Religion and the Decline of Magic*
Thucydides's *The History of the Peloponnesian War*
Frederick Jackson Turner's *The Significance of the Frontier in American History*
Odd Arne Westad's *The Global Cold War: Third World Interventions And The Making Of Our Times*

The Macat Library By Discipline

LITERATURE

Chinua Achebe's *An Image of Africa: Racism in Conrad's Heart of Darkness*
Roland Barthes's *Mythologies*
Homi K. Bhabha's *The Location of Culture*
Judith Butler's *Gender Trouble*
Simone De Beauvoir's *The Second Sex*
Ferdinand De Saussure's *Course in General Linguistics*
T. S. Eliot's *The Sacred Wood: Essays on Poetry and Criticism*
Zora Neale Huston's *Characteristics of Negro Expression*
Toni Morrison's *Playing in the Dark: Whiteness in the American Literary Imagination*
Edward Said's *Orientalism*
Gayatri Chakravorty Spivak's *Can the Subaltern Speak?*
Mary Wollstonecraft's *A Vindication of the Rights of Women*
Virginia Woolf's *A Room of One's Own*

PHILOSOPHY

Elizabeth Anscombe's *Modern Moral Philosophy*
Hannah Arendt's *The Human Condition*
Aristotle's *Metaphysics*
Aristotle's *Nicomachean Ethics*
Edmund Gettier's *Is Justified True Belief Knowledge?*
Georg Wilhelm Friedrich Hegel's *Phenomenology of Spirit*
David Hume's *Dialogues Concerning Natural Religion*
David Hume's *The Enquiry for Human Understanding*
Immanuel Kant's *Religion within the Boundaries of Mere Reason*
Immanuel Kant's *Critique of Pure Reason*
Søren Kierkegaard's *The Sickness Unto Death*
Søren Kierkegaard's *Fear and Trembling*
C. S. Lewis's *The Abolition of Man*
Alasdair MacIntyre's *After Virtue*
Marcus Aurelius's *Meditations*
Friedrich Nietzsche's *On the Genealogy of Morality*
Friedrich Nietzsche's *Beyond Good and Evil*
Plato's *Republic*
Plato's *Symposium*
Jean-Jacques Rousseau's *The Social Contract*
Gilbert Ryle's *The Concept of Mind*
Baruch Spinoza's *Ethics*
Sun Tzu's *The Art of War*
Ludwig Wittgenstein's *Philosophical Investigations*

POLITICS

Benedict Anderson's *Imagined Communities*
Aristotle's *Politics*
Bernard Bailyn's *The Ideological Origins of the American Revolution*
Edmund Burke's *Reflections on the Revolution in France*
John C. Calhoun's *A Disquisition on Government*
Ha-Joon Chang's *Kicking Away the Ladder*
Hamid Dabashi's *Iran: A People Interrupted*
Hamid Dabashi's *Theology of Discontent: The Ideological Foundation of the Islamic Revolution in Iran*
Robert Dahl's *Democracy and its Critics*
Robert Dahl's *Who Governs?*
David Brion Davis's *The Problem of Slavery in the Age of Revolution*

Alexis De Tocqueville's *Democracy in America*
James Ferguson's *The Anti-Politics Machine*
Frank Dikotter's *Mao's Great Famine*
Sheila Fitzpatrick's *Everyday Stalinism*
Eric Foner's *Reconstruction: America's Unfinished Revolution, 1863-1877*
Milton Friedman's *Capitalism and Freedom*
Francis Fukuyama's *The End of History and the Last Man*
John Lewis Gaddis's *We Now Know: Rethinking Cold War History*
Ernest Gellner's *Nations and Nationalism*
David Graeber's *Debt: the First 5000 Years*
Antonio Gramsci's *The Prison Notebooks*
Alexander Hamilton, John Jay & James Madison's *The Federalist Papers*
Friedrich Hayek's *The Road to Serfdom*
Christopher Hill's *The World Turned Upside Down*
Thomas Hobbes's *Leviathan*
John A. Hobson's *Imperialism: A Study*
Samuel P. Huntington's *The Clash of Civilizations and the Remaking of World Order*
Tony Judt's *Postwar: A History of Europe Since 1945*
David C. Kang's *China Rising: Peace, Power and Order in East Asia*
Paul Kennedy's *The Rise and Fall of Great Powers*
Robert Keohane's *After Hegemony*
Martin Luther King Jr.'s *Why We Can't Wait*
Henry Kissinger's *World Order: Reflections on the Character of Nations and the Course of History*
John Locke's *Two Treatises of Government*
Niccolò Machiavelli's *The Prince*
Thomas Robert Malthus's *An Essay on the Principle of Population*
Mahmood Mamdani's *Citizen and Subject: Contemporary Africa And The Legacy Of
Late Colonialism*
Karl Marx's *Capital*
John Stuart Mill's *On Liberty*
John Stuart Mill's *Utilitarianism*
Hans Morgenthau's *Politics Among Nations*
Thomas Paine's *Common Sense*
Thomas Paine's *Rights of Man*
Thomas Piketty's *Capital in the Twenty-First Century*
Robert D. Putman's *Bowling Alone*
John Rawls's *Theory of Justice*
Jean-Jacques Rousseau's *The Social Contract*
Theda Skocpol's *States and Social Revolutions*
Adam Smith's *The Wealth of Nations*
Sun Tzu's *The Art of War*
Henry David Thoreau's *Civil Disobedience*
Thucydides's *The History of the Peloponnesian War*
Kenneth Waltz's *Theory of International Politics*
Max Weber's *Politics as a Vocation*
Odd Arne Westad's *The Global Cold War: Third World Interventions And The Making Of Our Times*

POSTCOLONIAL STUDIES

Roland Barthes's *Mythologies*
Frantz Fanon's *Black Skin, White Masks*
Homi K. Bhabha's *The Location of Culture*
Gustavo Gutiérrez's *A Theology of Liberation*
Edward Said's *Orientalism*
Gayatri Chakravorty Spivak's *Can the Subaltern Speak?*

PSYCHOLOGY

Gordon Allport's *The Nature of Prejudice*
Alan Baddeley & Graham Hitch's *Aggression: A Social Learning Analysis*
Albert Bandura's *Aggression: A Social Learning Analysis*
Leon Festinger's *A Theory of Cognitive Dissonance*
Sigmund Freud's *The Interpretation of Dreams*
Betty Friedan's *The Feminine Mystique*
Michael R. Gottfredson & Travis Hirschi's *A General Theory of Crime*
Eric Hoffer's *The True Believer: Thoughts on the Nature of Mass Movements*
William James's *Principles of Psychology*
Elizabeth Loftus's *Eyewitness Testimony*
A. H. Maslow's *A Theory of Human Motivation*
Stanley Milgram's *Obedience to Authority*
Steven Pinker's *The Better Angels of Our Nature*
Oliver Sacks's *The Man Who Mistook His Wife For a Hat*
Richard Thaler & Cass Sunstein's *Nudge: Improving Decisions About Health, Wealth and Happiness*
Amos Tversky's *Judgment under Uncertainty: Heuristics and Biases*
Philip Zimbardo's *The Lucifer Effect*

SCIENCE

Rachel Carson's *Silent Spring*
William Cronon's *Nature's Metropolis: Chicago And The Great West*
Alfred W. Crosby's *The Columbian Exchange*
Charles Darwin's *On the Origin of Species*
Richard Dawkin's *The Selfish Gene*
Thomas Kuhn's *The Structure of Scientific Revolutions*
Geoffrey Parker's *Global Crisis: War, Climate Change and Catastrophe in the Seventeenth Century*
Mathis Wackernagel & William Rees's *Our Ecological Footprint*

SOCIOLOGY

Michelle Alexander's *The New Jim Crow: Mass Incarceration in the Age of Colorblindness*
Gordon Allport's *The Nature of Prejudice*
Albert Bandura's *Aggression: A Social Learning Analysis*
Hanna Batatu's *The Old Social Classes And The Revolutionary Movements Of Iraq*
Ha-Joon Chang's *Kicking Away the Ladder*
W. E. B. Du Bois's *The Souls of Black Folk*
Émile Durkheim's *On Suicide*
Frantz Fanon's *Black Skin, White Masks*
Frantz Fanon's *The Wretched of the Earth*
Eric Foner's *Reconstruction: America's Unfinished Revolution, 1863-1877*
Eugene Genovese's *Roll, Jordan, Roll: The World the Slaves Made*
Jack Goldstone's *Revolution and Rebellion in the Early Modern World*
Antonio Gramsci's *The Prison Notebooks*
Richard Herrnstein & Charles A Murray's *The Bell Curve: Intelligence and Class Structure in American Life*
Eric Hoffer's *The True Believer: Thoughts on the Nature of Mass Movements*
Jane Jacobs's *The Death and Life of Great American Cities*
Robert Lucas's *Why Doesn't Capital Flow from Rich to Poor Countries?*
Jay Macleod's *Ain't No Makin' It: Aspirations and Attainment in a Low Income Neighborhood*
Elaine May's *Homeward Bound: American Families in the Cold War Era*
Douglas McGregor's *The Human Side of Enterprise*
C. Wright Mills's *The Sociological Imagination*

Thomas Piketty's *Capital in the Twenty-First Century*
Robert D. Putman's *Bowling Alone*
David Riesman's *The Lonely Crowd: A Study of the Changing American Character*
Edward Said's *Orientalism*
Joan Wallach Scott's *Gender and the Politics of History*
Theda Skocpol's *States and Social Revolutions*
Max Weber's *The Protestant Ethic and the Spirit of Capitalism*

THEOLOGY

Augustine's *Confessions*
Benedict's *Rule of St Benedict*
Gustavo Gutiérrez's *A Theology of Liberation*
Carole Hillenbrand's *The Crusades: Islamic Perspectives*
David Hume's *Dialogues Concerning Natural Religion*
Immanuel Kant's *Religion within the Boundaries of Mere Reason*
Ernst Kantorowicz's *The King's Two Bodies: A Study in Medieval Political Theology*
Søren Kierkegaard's *The Sickness Unto Death*
C. S. Lewis's *The Abolition of Man*
Saba Mahmood's *The Politics of Piety: The Islamic Revival and the Feminist Subject*
Baruch Spinoza's *Ethics*
Keith Thomas's *Religion and the Decline of Magic*

Macat Disciplines

Access the greatest ideas and thinkers across entire disciplines, including

AFRICANA STUDIES

Chinua Achebe's *An Image of Africa: Racism in Conrad's Heart of Darkness*

W. E. B. Du Bois's *The Souls of Black Folk*

Zora Neale Hurston's *Characteristics of Negro Expression*

Martin Luther King Jr.'s *Why We Can't Wait*

Toni Morrison's *Playing in the Dark: Whiteness in the American Literary Imagination*

Macat analyses are available from all good bookshops and libraries.

Access hundreds of analyses through one, multimedia tool.
Join free for one month **library.macat.com**

Macat Disciplines

Access the greatest ideas and thinkers across entire disciplines, including

FEMINISM, GENDER AND QUEER STUDIES

Simone De Beauvoir's
The Second Sex

Michel Foucault's
History of Sexuality

Betty Friedan's
The Feminine Mystique

Saba Mahmood's
*The Politics of Piety:
The Islamic Revival and
the Feminist Subject*

Joan Wallach Scott's
*Gender and the
Politics of History*

Mary Wollstonecraft's
*A Vindication of the
Rights of Woman*

Virginia Woolf's
A Room of One's Own

Judith Butler's
Gender Trouble

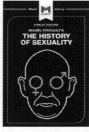

Macat Disciplines

Access the greatest ideas and thinkers across entire disciplines, including

INEQUALITY

Ha-Joon Chang's, *Kicking Away the Ladder*
David Graeber's, *Debt: The First 5000 Years*
Robert E. Lucas's, *Why Doesn't Capital Flow from Rich To Poor Countries?*
Thomas Piketty's, *Capital in the Twenty-First Century*
Amartya Sen's, *Inequality Re-Examined*
Mahbub Ul Haq's, *Reflections on Human Development*

Macat analyses are available from all good bookshops and libraries.

Access hundreds of analyses through one, multimedia tool.

Join free for one month **library.macat.com**

Macat Disciplines

Access the greatest ideas and thinkers across entire disciplines, including

CRIMINOLOGY

Michelle Alexander's
*The New Jim Crow:
Mass Incarceration in the
Age of Colorblindness*

**Michael R. Gottfredson
& Travis Hirschi's**
A General Theory of Crime

Elizabeth Loftus's
Eyewitness Testimony

**Richard Herrnstein
& Charles A. Murray's**
*The Bell Curve: Intelligence and
Class Structure in American Life*

Jay Macleod's
*Ain't No Makin' It:
Aspirations and Attainment in a
Low-Income Neighborhood*

Philip Zimbardo's
The Lucifer Effect

Macat analyses are available from all good bookshops and libraries.

Access hundreds of analyses through one, multimedia tool.
Join free for one month **library.macat.com**

Macat Disciplines

Access the greatest ideas and thinkers across entire disciplines, including

Postcolonial Studies

Roland Barthes's *Mythologies*
Frantz Fanon's *Black Skin, White Masks*
Homi K. Bhabha's *The Location of Culture*
Gustavo Gutiérrez's *A Theology of Liberation*
Edward Said's *Orientalism*
Gayatri Chakravorty Spivak's *Can the Subaltern Speak?*

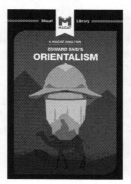

Macat analyses are available from all good bookshops and libraries.

Access hundreds of analyses through one, multimedia tool.
Join free for one month **library.macat.com**

Macat Pairs

*Analyse historical and modern issues
from opposite sides of an argument.
Pairs include:*

HOW TO RUN AN ECONOMY

John Maynard Keynes's
*The General Theory OF Employment,
Interest and Money*

Classical economics suggests that market economies
are self-correcting in times of recession or depression,
and tend toward full employment and output. But
English economist John Maynard Keynes disagrees.

In his ground-breaking 1936 study *The General
Theory*, Keynes argues that traditional economics
has misunderstood the causes of unemployment.
Employment is not determined by the price of labor;
it is directly linked to demand. Keynes believes market
economies are by nature unstable, and so require
government intervention. Spurred on by the social
catastrophe of the Great Depression of the 1930s,
he sets out to revolutionize the way the world thinks

Milton Friedman's
The Role of Monetary Policy

Friedman's 1968 paper changed the course of
economic theory. In just 17 pages, he demolished
existing theory and outlined an effective alternate
monetary policy designed to secure 'high employment,
stable prices and rapid growth.'

Friedman demonstrated that monetary policy plays
a vital role in broader economic stability and argued
that economists got their monetary policy wrong
in the 1950s and 1960s by misunderstanding the
relationship between inflation and unemployment.
Previous generations of economists had believed
that governments could permanently decrease
unemployment by permitting inflation—and vice versa.
Friedman's most original contribution was to show that
this supposed trade-off is an illusion that only works in
the short term.

Macat analyses are available from all good bookshops and libraries.

Access hundreds of analyses through one, multimedia tool.
Join free for one month **library.macat.com**

Macat Disciplines

Access the greatest ideas and thinkers across entire disciplines, including

THE FUTURE OF DEMOCRACY

Robert A. Dahl's, *Democracy and Its Critics*
Robert A. Dahl's, *Who Governs?*
Alexis De Toqueville's, *Democracy in America*
Niccolò Machiavelli's, *The Prince*
John Stuart Mill's, *On Liberty*
Robert D. Putnam's, *Bowling Alone*
Jean-Jacques Rousseau's, *The Social Contract*
Henry David Thoreau's, *Civil Disobedience*

Macat Disciplines

*Access the greatest ideas and thinkers
across entire disciplines, including*

TOTALITARIANISM

Sheila Fitzpatrick's, *Everyday Stalinism*
Ian Kershaw's, *The "Hitler Myth"*
Timothy Snyder's, *Bloodlands*

Macat analyses are available from all good bookshops and libraries.

Access hundreds of analyses through one, multimedia tool.
Join free for one month **library.macat.com**

Macat Pairs

Analyse historical and modern issues from opposite sides of an argument. Pairs include:

MACAT

MACAT

INTERNATIONAL RELATIONS IN THE 21ST CENTURY

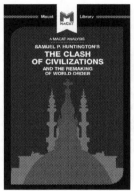

Samuel P. Huntington's
The Clash of Civilisations

In his highly influential 1996 book, Huntington offers a vision of a post-Cold War world in which conflict takes place not between competing ideologies but between cultures. The worst clash, he argues, will be between the Islamic world and the West: the West's arrogance and belief that its culture is a "gift" to the world will come into conflict with Islam's obstinacy and concern that its culture is under attack from a morally decadent "other."

Clash inspired much debate between different political schools of thought. But its greatest impact came in helping define American foreign policy in the wake of the 2001 terrorist attacks in New York and Washington.

Francis Fukuyama's
The End of History and the Last Man

Published in 1992, *The End of History and the Last Man* argues that capitalist democracy is the final destination for all societies. Fukuyama believed democracy triumphed during the Cold War because it lacks the "fundamental contradictions" inherent in communism and satisfies our yearning for freedom and equality. Democracy therefore marks the endpoint in the evolution of ideology, and so the "end of history." There will still be "events," but no fundamental change in ideology.

Macat Pairs

Analyse historical and modern issues from opposite sides of an argument. Pairs include:

ARE WE FUNDAMENTALLY GOOD - OR BAD?

Steven Pinker's
The Better Angels of Our Nature

Stephen Pinker's gloriously optimistic 2011 book argues that, despite humanity's biological tendency toward violence, we are, in fact, less violent today than ever before. To prove his case, Pinker lays out pages of detailed statistical evidence. For him, much of the credit for the decline goes to the eighteenth-century Enlightenment movement, whose ideas of liberty, tolerance, and respect for the value of human life filtered down through society and affected how people thought. That psychological change led to behavioral change—and overall we became more peaceful. Critics countered that humanity could never overcome the biological urge toward violence; others argued that Pinker's statistics were flawed.

Philip Zimbardo's
The Lucifer Effect

Some psychologists believe those who commit cruelty are innately evil. Zimbardo disagrees. In *The Lucifer Effect*, he argues that sometimes good people do evil things simply because of the situations they find themselves in, citing many historical examples to illustrate his point. Zimbardo details his 1971 Stanford prison experiment, where ordinary volunteers playing guards in a mock prison rapidly became abusive. But he also describes the tortures committed by US army personnel in Iraq's Abu Ghraib prison in 2003—and how he himself testified in defence of one of those guards. committed by US army personnel in Iraq's Abu Ghraib prison in 2003—and how he himself testified in defence of one of those guards.

Macat analyses are available from all good bookshops and libraries.

Access hundreds of analyses through one, multimedia tool.
Join free for one month **library.macat.com**

Printed in the United States
by Baker & Taylor Publisher Services